GW00602843

NOTES
POCKET

KITCHEN & HOME
DIARY
2016

WEEK-TO-VIEW
DIARY WITH RECIPES

Name

Address

Postcode

☎ Home

☎ Mobile

Email

In case of emergency contact:

Name

☎ Tel.

www.kitchenandhomediary.co.uk

While every care has been taken in compiling the information in this diary, the publishers cannot accept responsibility for any errors, inadvertent or not, that may be found or may occur at some time in the future owing to changes in legislation or any other reason.

© Eaglemoss Consumer Publications Ltd 2015

Published by Eaglemoss Consumer Publications Ltd.

Reminders

National insurance number

NHS number

Blood group

Passport number

Vehicle registration number

Driving licence number

Car insurance renewal date

Road tax renewal date

MOT date

Car service date

House insurance renewal date

TV licence renewal date

Other

Other

Other

Other

Notes

Useful contacts

Airport

Bank

Breakdown service

Building society

Chemist

Childminder/nursery

Chiropodist

Council

Credit card emergency

Dentist

Doctor

Electrician

Electricity provider

Garage

Gas engineer

Gas provider

Hairdresser

Hospital

NHS direct   111

Optician

Plumber

Police (non-emergency number)   101

School

Solicitor

Taxi

Vet

Water provider

Work

Other

Personal contacts

Name

Address

📞 Telephone

   Mobile 1

   Mobile 2

   Work

Email 1

Email 2

Name

Address

📞 Telephone

   Mobile 1

   Mobile 2

   Work

Email 1

Email 2

Name

Address

📞 Telephone

   Mobile 1

   Mobile 2

   Work

Email 1

Email 2

Name

Address

📞 Telephone

   Mobile 1

   Mobile 2

   Work

Email 1

Email 2

Name

Address

📞 Telephone

   Mobile 1

   Mobile 2

   Work

Email 1

Email 2

Name

Address

📞 Telephone

   Mobile 1

   Mobile 2

   Work

Email 1

Email 2

Name

Address

📞 Telephone

    Mobile 1

    Mobile 2

    Work

Email 1

Email 2

Name

Address

📞 Telephone

    Mobile 1

    Mobile 2

    Work

Email 1

Email 2

Name

Address

📞 Telephone

    Mobile 1

    Mobile 2

    Work

Email 1

Email 2

Name

Address

📞 Telephone

    Mobile 1

    Mobile 2

    Work

Email 1

Email 2

Name

Address

📞 Telephone

    Mobile 1

    Mobile 2

    Work

Email 1

Email 2

Name

Address

📞 Telephone

    Mobile 1

    Mobile 2

    Work

Email 1

Email 2

Personal contacts

Name	Name
Address	Address
☎ Telephone	☎ Telephone
Mobile 1	Mobile 1
Mobile 2	Mobile 2
Work	Work
Email 1	Email 1
Email 2	Email 2
Name	Name
Address	Address
☎ Telephone	☎ Telephone
Mobile 1	Mobile 1
Mobile 2	Mobile 2
Work	Work
Email 1	Email 1
Email 2	Email 2
Name	Name
Address	Address
☎ Telephone	☎ Telephone
Mobile 1	Mobile 1
Mobile 2	Mobile 2
Work	Work
Email 1	Email 1
Email 2	Email 2

Name

Address

📞 Telephone

   Mobile 1

   Mobile 2

   Work

Email 1

Email 2

Name

Address

📞 Telephone

   Mobile 1

   Mobile 2

   Work

Email 1

Email 2

Name

Address

📞 Telephone

   Mobile 1

   Mobile 2

   Work

Email 1

Email 2

Name

Address

📞 Telephone

   Mobile 1

   Mobile 2

   Work

Email 1

Email 2

Name

Address

📞 Telephone

   Mobile 1

   Mobile 2

   Work

Email 1

Email 2

Name

Address

📞 Telephone

   Mobile 1

   Mobile 2

   Work

Email 1

Email 2

Personal contacts

Name

Address

📞 Telephone

   Mobile 1

   Mobile 2

   Work

Email 1

Email 2

Name

Address

📞 Telephone

   Mobile 1

   Mobile 2

   Work

Email 1

Email 2

Name

Address

📞 Telephone

   Mobile 1

   Mobile 2

   Work

Email 1

Email 2

Name

Address

📞 Telephone

   Mobile 1

   Mobile 2

   Work

Email 1

Email 2

Name

Address

📞 Telephone

   Mobile 1

   Mobile 2

   Work

Email 1

Email 2

Name

Address

📞 Telephone

   Mobile 1

   Mobile 2

   Work

Email 1

Email 2

Name	Name
Address	Address

📞 Telephone

   Mobile 1

   Mobile 2

   Work

Email 1

Email 2

📞 Telephone

   Mobile 1

   Mobile 2

   Work

Email 1

Email 2

Name	Name
Address	Address

📞 Telephone

   Mobile 1

   Mobile 2

   Work

Email 1

Email 2

📞 Telephone

   Mobile 1

   Mobile 2

   Work

Email 1

Email 2

Name	Name
Address	Address

📞 Telephone

   Mobile 1

   Mobile 2

   Work

Email 1

Email 2

📞 Telephone

   Mobile 1

   Mobile 2

   Work

Email 1

Email 2

Year planner 2016

January		February		March	
1 Fri	BANK HOLIDAY	1 Mon		1 Tue	
2 Sat		2 Tue		2 Wed	
3 Sun		3 Wed		3 Thu	
4 Mon	BANK HOLIDAY SCOTLAND	4 Thu		4 Fri	
5 Tue		5 Fri		5 Sat	
6 Wed		6 Sat		6 Sun	
7 Thu		7 Sun		7 Mon	
8 Fri		8 Mon		8 Tue	
9 Sat		9 Tue		9 Wed	
10 Sun		10 Wed		10 Thu	
11 Mon		11 Thu		11 Fri	
12 Tue		12 Fri		12 Sat	
13 Wed		13 Sat		13 Sun	
14 Thu		14 Sun		14 Mon	
15 Fri		15 Mon		15 Tue	
16 Sat		16 Tue		16 Wed	
17 Sun		17 Wed		17 Thu	BANK HOLIDAY N IRELAND
18 Mon		18 Thu		18 Fri	
19 Tue		19 Fri		19 Sat	
20 Wed		20 Sat		20 Sun	
21 Thu		21 Sun		21 Mon	
22 Fri		22 Mon		22 Tue	
23 Sat		23 Tue		23 Wed	
24 Sun		24 Wed		24 Thu	
25 Mon		25 Thu		25 Fri	BANK HOLIDAY
26 Tue		26 Fri		26 Sat	
27 Wed		27 Sat		27 Sun	
28 Thu		28 Sun		28 Mon	BANK HOLIDAY
29 Fri		29 Mon		29 Tue	
30 Sat				30 Wed	
31 Sun				31 Thu	

April	May	June
1 Fri	1 Sun	1 Wed
2 Sat	2 Mon BANK HOLIDAY	2 Thu
3 Sun	3 Tue	3 Fri
4 Mon	4 Wed	4 Sat
5 Tue	5 Thu	5 Sun
6 Wed	6 Fri	6 Mon
7 Thu	7 Sat	7 Tue
8 Fri	8 Sun	8 Wed
9 Sat	9 Mon	9 Thu
10 Sun	10 Tue	10 Fri
11 Mon	11 Wed	11 Sat
12 Tue	12 Thu	12 Sun
13 Wed	13 Fri	13 Mon
14 Thu	14 Sat	14 Tue
15 Fri	15 Sun	15 Wed
16 Sat	16 Mon	16 Thu
17 Sun	17 Tue	17 Fri
18 Mon	18 Wed	18 Sat
19 Tue	19 Thu	19 Sun
20 Wed	20 Fri	20 Mon
21 Thu	21 Sat	21 Tue
22 Fri	22 Sun	22 Wed
23 Sat	23 Mon	23 Thu
24 Sun	24 Tue	24 Fri
25 Mon	25 Wed	25 Sat
26 Tue	26 Thu	26 Sun
27 Wed	27 Fri	27 Mon
28 Thu	28 Sat	28 Tue
29 Fri	29 Sun	29 Wed
30 Sat	30 Mon BANK HOLIDAY	30 Thu
	31 Tue	

Year planner 2016

July		August		September	
1	Fri	1	Mon BANK HOLIDAY SCOTLAND	1	Thu
2	Sat	2	Tue	2	Fri
3	Sun	3	Wed	3	Sat
4	Mon	4	Thu	4	Sun
5	Tue	5	Fri	5	Mon
6	Wed	6	Sat	6	Tue
7	Thu	7	Sun	7	Wed
8	Fri	8	Mon	8	Thu
9	Sat	9	Tue	9	Fri
10	Sun	10	Wed	10	Sat
11	Mon	11	Thu	11	Sun
12	Tue BANK HOLIDAY N IRELAND	12	Fri	12	Mon
13	Wed	13	Sat	13	Tue
14	Thu	14	Sun	14	Wed
15	Fri	15	Mon	15	Thu
16	Sat	16	Tue	16	Fri
17	Sun	17	Wed	17	Sat
18	Mon	18	Thu	18	Sun
19	Tue	19	Fri	19	Mon
20	Wed	20	Sat	20	Tue
21	Thu	21	Sun	21	Wed
22	Fri	22	Mon	22	Thu
23	Sat	23	Tue	23	Fri
24	Sun	24	Wed	24	Sat
25	Mon	25	Thu	25	Sun
26	Tue	26	Fri	26	Mon
27	Wed	27	Sat	27	Tue
28	Thu	28	Sun	28	Wed
29	Fri	29	Mon BANK HOLIDAY	29	Thu
30	Sat	30	Tue	30	Fri
31	Sun	31	Wed		

October	November	December
1 Sat	1 Tue	1 Thu
2 Sun	2 Wed	2 Fri
3 Mon	3 Thu	3 Sat
4 Tue	4 Fri	4 Sun
5 Wed	5 Sat	5 Mon
6 Thu	6 Sun	6 Tue
7 Fri	7 Mon	7 Wed
8 Sat	8 Tue	8 Thu
9 Sun	9 Wed	9 Fri
10 Mon	10 Thu	10 Sat
11 Tue	11 Fri	11 Sun
12 Wed	12 Sat	12 Mon
13 Thu	13 Sun	13 Tue
14 Fri	14 Mon	14 Wed
15 Sat	15 Tue	15 Thu
16 Sun	16 Wed	16 Fri
17 Mon	17 Thu	17 Sat
18 Tue	18 Fri	18 Sun
19 Wed	19 Sat	19 Mon
20 Thu	20 Sun	20 Tue
21 Fri	21 Mon	21 Wed
22 Sat	22 Tue	22 Thu
23 Sun	23 Wed	23 Fri
24 Mon	24 Thu	24 Sat
25 Tue	25 Fri	25 Sun
26 Wed	26 Sat	26 Mon BANK HOLIDAY
27 Thu	27 Sun	27 Tue BANK HOLIDAY
28 Fri	28 Mon	28 Wed
29 Sat	29 Tue	29 Thu
30 Sun	30 Wed	30 Fri
31 Mon		31 Sat

2015

January
Mon		5	12	19	26
Tue		6	13	20	27
Wed		7	14	21	28
Thu	1	8	15	22	29
Fri	2	9	16	23	30
Sat	3	10	17	24	31
Sun	4	11	18	25	

February
Mon		2	9	16	23
Tue		3	10	17	24
Wed		4	11	18	25
Thu		5	12	19	26
Fri		6	13	20	27
Sat		7	14	21	28
Sun	1	8	15	22	

March
Mon		2	9	16	23	30
Tue		3	10	17	24	31
Wed		4	11	18	25	
Thu		5	12	19	26	
Fri		6	13	20	27	
Sat		7	14	21	28	
Sun	1	8	15	22	29	

April
Mon		6	13	20	27
Tue		7	14	21	28
Wed	1	8	15	22	29
Thu	2	9	16	23	30
Fri	3	10	17	24	
Sat	4	11	18	25	
Sun	5	12	19	26	

May
Mon		4	11	18	25
Tue		5	12	19	26
Wed		6	13	20	27
Thu		7	14	21	28
Fri	1	8	15	22	29
Sat	2	9	16	23	30
Sun	3	10	17	24	31

June
Mon	1	8	15	22	29
Tue	2	9	16	23	30
Wed	3	10	17	24	
Thu	4	11	18	25	
Fri	5	12	19	26	
Sat	6	13	20	27	
Sun	7	14	21	28	

July
Mon		6	13	20	27
Tue		7	14	21	28
Wed	1	8	15	22	29
Thu	2	9	16	23	30
Fri	3	10	17	24	31
Sat	4	11	18	25	
Sun	5	12	19	26	

August
Mon		3	10	17	24	31
Tue		4	11	18	25	
Wed		5	12	19	26	
Thu		6	13	20	27	
Fri		7	14	21	28	
Sat	1	8	15	22	29	
Sun	2	9	16	23	30	

September
Mon		7	14	21	28
Tue	1	8	15	22	29
Wed	2	9	16	23	30
Thu	3	10	17	24	
Fri	4	11	18	25	
Sat	5	12	19	26	
Sun	6	13	20	27	

October
Mon		5	12	19	26
Tue		6	13	20	27
Wed		7	14	21	28
Thu	1	8	15	22	29
Fri	2	9	16	23	30
Sat	3	10	17	24	31
Sun	4	11	18	25	

November
Mon		2	9	16	23	30
Tue		3	10	17	24	
Wed		4	11	18	25	
Thu		5	12	19	26	
Fri		6	13	20	27	
Sat		7	14	21	28	
Sun	1	8	15	22	29	

December
Mon		7	14	21	28
Tue	1	8	15	22	29
Wed	2	9	16	23	30
Thu	3	10	17	24	31
Fri	4	11	18	25	
Sat	5	12	19	26	
Sun	6	13	20	27	

2017

January
Mon		2	9	16	23	30
Tue		3	10	17	24	31
Wed		4	11	18	25	
Thu		5	12	19	26	
Fri		6	13	20	27	
Sat		7	14	21	28	
Sun	1	8	15	22	29	

February
Mon		6	13	20	27
Tue		7	14	21	28
Wed	1	8	15	22	
Thu	2	9	16	23	
Fri	3	10	17	24	
Sat	4	11	18	25	
Sun	5	12	19	26	

March
Mon		6	13	20	27
Tue		7	14	21	28
Wed	1	8	15	22	29
Thu	2	9	16	23	30
Fri	3	10	17	24	31
Sat	4	11	18	25	
Sun	5	12	19	26	

April
Mon		3	10	17	24
Tue		4	11	18	25
Wed		5	12	19	26
Thu		6	13	20	27
Fri		7	14	21	28
Sat	1	8	15	22	29
Sun	2	9	16	23	30

May
Mon	1	8	15	22	29
Tue	2	9	16	23	30
Wed	3	10	17	24	31
Thu	4	11	18	25	
Fri	5	12	19	26	
Sat	6	13	20	27	
Sun	7	14	21	28	

June
Mon		5	12	19	26
Tue		6	13	20	27
Wed		7	14	21	28
Thu	1	8	15	22	29
Fri	2	9	16	23	30
Sat	3	10	17	24	
Sun	4	11	18	25	

July
Mon		3	10	17	24	31
Tue		4	11	18	25	
Wed		5	12	19	26	
Thu		6	13	20	27	
Fri		7	14	21	28	
Sat	1	8	15	22	29	
Sun	2	9	16	23	30	

August
Mon		7	14	21	28
Tue	1	8	15	22	29
Wed	2	9	16	23	30
Thu	3	10	17	24	31
Fri	4	11	18	25	
Sat	5	12	19	26	
Sun	6	13	20	27	

September
Mon		4	11	18	25
Tue		5	12	19	26
Wed		6	13	20	27
Thu		7	14	21	28
Fri	1	8	15	22	29
Sat	2	9	16	23	30
Sun	3	10	17	24	

October
Mon		2	9	16	23	30
Tue		3	10	17	24	31
Wed		4	11	18	25	
Thu		5	12	19	26	
Fri		6	13	20	27	
Sat		7	14	21	28	
Sun	1	8	15	22	29	

November
Mon		6	13	20	27
Tue		7	14	21	28
Wed	1	8	15	22	29
Thu	2	9	16	23	30
Fri	3	10	17	24	
Sat	4	11	18	25	
Sun	5	12	19	26	

December
Mon		4	11	18	25
Tue		5	12	19	26
Wed		6	13	20	27
Thu		7	14	21	28
Fri	1	8	15	22	29
Sat	2	9	16	23	30
Sun	3	10	17	24	31

2016

January

Mon	4	11	18	25
Tue	5	12	19	26
Wed	6	13	20	27
Thu	7	14	21	28
Fri	1	8	15	22	29
Sat	2	9	16	23	30
Sun	3	10	17	24	31

February

Mon	1	8	15	22	29
Tue	2	9	16	23	
Wed	3	10	17	24	
Thu	4	11	18	25	
Fri	5	12	19	26	
Sat	6	13	20	27	
Sun	7	14	21	28	

March

Mon		7	14	21	28
Tue	1	8	15	22	29
Wed	2	9	16	23	30
Thu	3	10	17	24	31
Fri	4	11	18	25	
Sat	5	12	19	26	
Sun	6	13	20	27	

April

Mon	4	11	18	25
Tue	5	12	19	26
Wed	6	13	20	27
Thu	7	14	21	28
Fri	1	8	15	22	29
Sat	2	9	16	23	30
Sun	3	10	17	24	

May

Mon		2	9	16	23	30
Tue		3	10	17	24	31
Wed		4	11	18	25	
Thu		5	12	19	26	
Fri		6	13	20	27	
Sat		7	14	21	28	
Sun	1	8	15	22	29	

June

Mon		6	13	20	27
Tue		7	14	21	28
Wed	1	8	15	22	29
Thu	2	9	16	23	30
Fri	3	10	17	24	
Sat	4	11	18	25	
Sun	5	12	19	26	

July

Mon	4	11	18	25
Tue	5	12	19	26
Wed	6	13	20	27
Thu	7	14	21	28
Fri	1	8	15	22	29
Sat	2	9	16	23	30
Sun	3	10	17	24	31

August

Mon	1	8	15	22	29
Tue	2	9	16	23	30
Wed	3	10	17	24	31
Thu	4	11	18	25	
Fri	5	12	19	26	
Sat	6	13	20	27	
Sun	7	14	21	28	

September

Mon		5	12	19	26
Tue		6	13	20	27
Wed		7	14	21	28
Thu	1	8	15	22	29
Fri	2	9	16	23	30
Sat	3	10	17	24	
Sun	4	11	18	25	

October

Mon		3	10	17	24	31
Tue		4	11	18	25	
Wed		5	12	19	26	
Thu		6	13	20	27	
Fri		7	14	21	28	
Sat	1	8	15	22	29	
Sun	2	9	16	23	30	

November

Mon		7	14	21	28
Tue	1	8	15	22	29
Wed	2	9	16	23	30
Thu	3	10	17	24	
Fri	4	11	18	25	
Sat	5	12	19	26	
Sun	6	13	20	27	

December

Mon		5	12	19	26
Tue		6	13	20	27
Wed		7	14	21	28
Thu	1	8	15	22	29
Fri	2	9	16	23	30
Sat	3	10	17	24	31
Sun	4	11	18	25	

Calendar dates

UK holidays †

	2016	2017
New Year	Jan 1	Jan 2*
New Year (Scotland)	Jan 1/4*	Jan 2/3*
St Patrick's Day (Northern Ireland)	Mar 17	Mar 17
Good Friday	Mar 25	Apr 14
Easter Monday (except Scotland)	Mar 28	Apr 17
Early Spring	May 2	May 1
Spring	May 30	May 29
Battle of the Boyne (Northern Ireland)	Jul 12	July 12
Summer (Scotland)	Aug 1	Aug 7
Summer (except Scotland)	Aug 29	Aug 28
Christmas Day	Dec 27*	Dec 25
Boxing Day	Dec 26	Dec 26

Notable dates

Burns' Night	Jan 25
Holocaust Memorial Day	Jan 27
Accession of Queen Elizabeth II	Feb 6
Chinese New Year – Year of the Monkey	Feb 8
Shrove Tuesday (Pancake Day)	Feb 9
St Valentine's Day	Feb 14
St David's Day (Wales)	Mar 1
Mother's Day	Mar 6
Commonwealth Day	Mar 14
St Patrick's Day (Ireland)	Mar 17
Birthday of Queen Elizabeth II	Apr 21
St George's Day (England)	Apr 23
World Red Cross/Red Crescent Day	May 8
Coronation Day	Jun 2
Queen's Official Birthday (t.b.c.)	Jun 11
Father's Day	Jun 19
Armed Forces' Day	Jun 25
St Swithin's Day	Jul 15
International Day of Peace	Sep 21
United Nations Day	Oct 24
Halloween	Oct 31
Armistice Day	Nov 11
Remembrance Sunday	Nov 13
Birthday of the Prince of Wales	Nov 14
St Andrew's Day (Scotland)	Nov 30

Religious dates

Christian

Epiphany	Jan 6
Ash Wednesday	Feb 10
Palm Sunday	Mar 20
Good Friday	Mar 25
Easter Day	Mar 27
Ascension Day	May 5
Whit Sunday, Pentecost	May 15
Trinity Sunday	May 22
Corpus Christi	May 26
Advent Sunday	Nov 27
Christmas Day	Dec 25

Buddhist

Parinirvana Day	Feb 8
Wesak (Buddha Day)	May 20
Bodhi Day (Buddha's enlightenment)	Dec 8

Hindu

Maha Shivaratri	Mar 8
Holi	Mar 23
Navaratri begins	Oct 1
Diwali begins (also celebrated by Sikhs)	Oct 30

Islamic

Ramadan begins	Jun 7
Eid Ul-Fitr	Jul 5
Eid Ul-Adha	Sep 11
Al-Hijra (New Year)	Oct 3
Milad un Nabi (Prophet's birthday)	Dec 12

Jewish

Purim begins	Mar 24
Pesach (Passover) begins	Apr 23
Shavuot (Pentecost) begins	Jun 12
Rosh Hashanah (Jewish New Year)	Oct 3
Yom Kippur (Day of Atonement)	Oct 12
Succoth (Tabernacles) begins	Oct 17
Chanukah begins	Dec 25

Sikh

These dates follow the Nanakshahi calendar

Birthday of Guru Gobind Singh	Jan 5
Vaisakhi	Apr 13
Birthday of Guru Nanak	Apr 14
Martyrdom of Guru Arjan Dev	Jun 16
Martyrdom of Guru Tegh Bahadur	Nov 24

Note: Many religious dates are based on the lunar calendar and, therefore, we cannot guarantee their accuracy.

†Bank Holiday dates can change *Substitute Bank Holidays –Scotland's New Year holiday falls on a Friday and Saturday in 2016; Christmas Day falls on a Sunday in 2016; New Year's Day falls on a Sunday in 2017.

Phases of the moon

● New moon			) First quarter		
	Day	H:M		Day	H:M
Jan	10	01:31	Jan	16	23:26
Feb	8	14:39	Feb	15	07:46
Mar	9	01:54	Mar	15	17:03
Apr	7	11:24	Apr	14	03:59
May	6	19:30	May	13	17:02
Jun	5	03:00	Jun	12	08:10
Jul	4	11:01	Jul	12	00:52
Aug	2	20:45	Aug	10	18:21
Sep	1	09:03	Sep	9	11:49
Oct	1	00:11	Oct	9	04:33
Oct	30	17:38	Nov	7	19:51
Nov	29	12:18	Dec	7	09:03
Dec	29	06:53			

○ Full moon			(Last quarter		
				Day	H:M
	Day	H:M	Jan	2	05:30
Jan	24	01:46	Feb	1	03:28
Feb	22	18:20	Mar	1	23:11
Mar	23	12:01	Mar	31	15:17
Apr	22	05:24	Apr	30	03:29
May	21	21:14	May	29	12:12
Jun	20	11:02	Jun	27	18:19
Jul	19	22:57	Jul	26	23:00
Aug	18	09:27	Aug	25	03:41
Sep	16	19:05	Sep	23	09:56
Oct	16	04:23	Oct	22	19:14
Nov	14	13:52	Nov	21	08:33
Dec	14	00:06	Dec	21	01:56

Seasons

	Month	Day	H:M
Vernal equinox			
Spring begins	Mar	20	04:30
Summer solstice			
Summer begins	June	20	22:34
Autumnal equinox			
Autumn begins	Sep	22	14:21
Winter solstice			
Winter begins	Dec	21	10:44

British summertime

▶ Clocks go forward
1 hour at 1am on
27 March

◀ Clocks go back
1 hour at 2am on
30 October

Websites

bankholidaydates.co.uk

when-is.com

© Crown copyright and/or database rights. Reproduced by permission of the Controller of Her Majesty's Stationery Office and the UK Hydrographic Office

Sunrise and sunset times Note: times vary – these are for London

Day	Rise H:M	Set H:M	Day	Rise H:M	Set H:M	Day	Rise H:M	Set H:M	Day	Rise H:M	Set H:M
January			**February**			**March**			**April**		
07	08:05	16:09	07	07:30	17:00	07	06:32	17:52	07	06:22	19:45
14	08:01	16:19	14	07:17	17:13	14	06:16	18:04	14	06:06	19:56
21	07:54	16:30	21	07:04	17:25	21	06:00	18:16	21	05:52	20:08
28	07:46	16:42	28	06:49	17:38	28	06:44	19:28	28	05:37	20:19
May			**June**			**July**			**August**		
07	05:21	20:34	07	04:45	21:14	07	04:53	21:18	07	05:34	20:37
14	05:10	20:45	14	04:43	21:19	14	05:00	21:12	14	05:45	20:24
21	05:00	20:55	21	04:43	21:22	21	05:09	21:04	21	05:56	20:10
28	04:52	21:04	28	04:46	21:21	28	05:19	20:54	28	06:07	19:55
September			**October**			**November**			**December**		
07	06:23	19:33	07	07:12	18:24	07	07:05	16:23	07	07:52	15:52
14	06:34	19:16	14	07:23	18:09	14	07:17	16:12	14	07:59	15:52
21	06:45	19:00	21	07:35	17:54	21	07:29	16:03	21	08:04	15:54
28	06:57	18:44	28	07:48	17:40	28	07:40	15:57	28	08:06	15:59

Height & weight chart

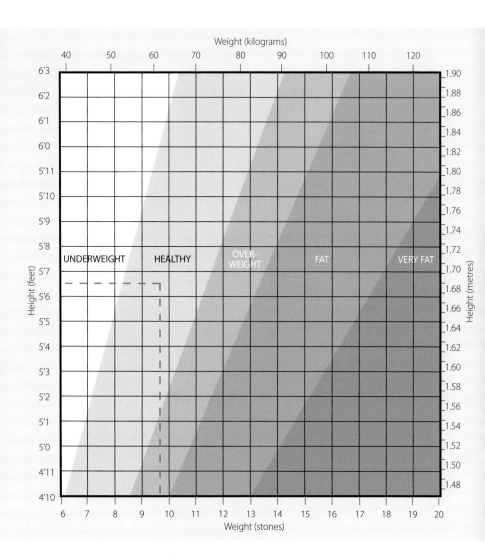

Weight (kilograms)

Height (feet) / Height (metres)

Regions: UNDERWEIGHT · HEALTHY · OVER-WEIGHT · FAT · VERY FAT

Weight (stones)

Guide for adult men and women

You may need to see your doctor if you are very underweight.

Desirable range for health.

Try to lose weight until you are in the desirable range.

To avoid potential health problems, it is important to lose weight.

Talk to your doctor or practice nurse. You can be referred to a dietitian.

Follow the lines from your weight and height (see example in dotted lines).
Where the two figures meet you'll find your weight level.

Metric conversions

Length

			To convert	multiply by
millimetre (mm)		= 0.0394in	mm to in	0.0394
centimetre (cm)	= 10mm	= 0.394in	cm to in	0.394
metre (m)	= 100cm	= 1.09yd	m to yd	1.09
kilometre (km)	= 1000m	= 0.621 mile	km to mi	0.621
inch (in)		= 2.54cm	in to cm	2.54
foot (ft)	= 12in	= 30.5cm	ft to cm	30.5
yard (yd)	= 3ft	= 0.914m	yd to m	0.914
mile (mi)	= 1760yd	= 1.61km	mi to km	1.61

Area

sq millimetre (mm)		= 0.00155sq in	mm^2 to in^2	0.00155
sq centimetre (cm)	= 100sq mm	= 0.155sq in	cm^2 to in^2	0.155
sq metre (m)	= 10,000sq cm	= 1.20sq yd	m^2 to yd^2	1.20
hectare (ha)	= 10,000sq m	= 2.47a	ha to a	2.47
sq kilometre (km)	= 100ha	= 0.386sq mile	km^2 to mi^2	0.386
sq inch (in)		= 6.45sq cm	in^2 to cm^2	6.45
sq foot (ft)	= 144sq in	= 0.0929sq m	ft^2 to m^2	0.0929
sq yard (yd)	= 9sq ft	= 0.836sq m	yd^2 to m^2	0.836
acre (a)	= 4840sq yd	= 4047sq m	a to m^2	4047
sq mile (mi)	= 640a	= 2.59sq km	mi^2 to km^2	2.59

Volume

cu centimetre (cm)	= 1000cu mm	= 0.0611cu in	cm^3 to in^3	0.0611
cu decimetre (dm)	= 1000cu cm	= 0.0353cu ft	dm^3 to ft^3	0.0353
cu metre (m)	= 1000cu dm	= 1.31cu yd	m^3 to yd^3	1.31
cu inch (in)		= 16.4cu cm	in^3 to cm^3	16.4
cu foot (ft)	= 1730cu in	= 28.4cu dm	ft^3 to dm^3	28.4
cu yard (yd)	= 27cu ft	= 0.765cu m	yd^3 to m^3	0.765

Capacity

1 millilitre (ml)		= 0.0352fl oz	ml to fl oz	0.0352
1 centilitre (cl)	= 10ml	= 0.352fl oz	cl to fl oz	0.352
1 litre (l)	= 100cl	= 1.76pt	l to pt	1.76
1 fluid ounce (fl oz)		= 28.4ml	fl oz to ml	28.4
1 gill (gi)	= 5fl oz	= 14.2cl	gi to cl	14.2
1 pint (pt)	= 20fl oz	= 0.568l	pt to l	0.568
1 quart (qt)	= 2pt	= 1.14l	qt to l	1.14
1 gallon (gal)	= 4qt	= 4.55l	gal to l	4.55

Weight

1 gram (g)	= 1000mg	= 0.0353oz	g to oz	0.0353
1 kilogram (kg)	= 1000g	= 2.20lb	kg to lb	2.20
1 tonne (t)	= 1000kg	= 0.984 ton	tonne to ton	0.984
1 ounce (oz)	= 438 grains	= 28.3g	oz to g	28.3
1 pound (lb)	= 16oz	= 0.454kg	lb to kg	0.454
1 stone (st)	= 14lb	= 6.35kg	st to kg	6.35
1 ton (t)	= 160st	= 1.02 tonne	ton to tonne	1.02

Cook's information

Dry weight conversions

grams (g)	ounces (oz)
15	½
25	1
50	2
75	3
110	4 (¼lb)
150	5
175	6
200	7
225	8 (½lb)
250	9
275	10
300	11
350	12 (¾lb)
375	13
400	14
425	15
450	16 (1lb)
500	1lb 2oz
680	1½lb
750	1lb 10oz
900	2lb

These quantities are not exact, but they have been calculated to give proportionately correct measurements.

Liquid conversions

millilitres (ml)	fluid ounces (fl oz)	US cups
15	½	1 tbsp (level)
30	1	⅛
60	2	¼
90	3	⅜
125	4	½
150	5 (¼ pint)	⅔
175	6	¾
225	8	1
300	10 (½ pint)	1¼
350	12	1½
450	16	2
500	18	2¼
600	20 (1 pint)	2½
900	1½ pints	3¾
1 litre	1¾ pints	1 quart (4 cups)
1.25 litres	2 pints	1¼ quarts
1.5 litres	2½ pints	3 US pints
2 litres	3½ pints	2 quarts

These quantities are not exact, but they have been calculated to give proportionately correct measurements.

Reference intake (RI)

Energy (calories)	2,000
Fat (g)	70
of which saturates (g)	20
Carbohydrate (g)	260
of which total sugars (g)	90
Protein (g)	50
Salt (g)	6

Spoon measures

1 tablespoon	=	3 level teaspoons
1 level tablespoon	=	15ml
1 level teaspoon	=	5ml

If greater accuracy is not required:

1 rounded teaspoon	=	2 level teaspoons
1 heaped teaspoon	=	3 level teaspoons or 1 level tablespoon

Grilling times: fish

	minutes each side
Cod (steak)	5–6
Dover sole (fillet)	2–3
Halibut (steak)	5–6
Herring (whole)	4–5
Mackerel (whole)	6–7
Monkfish (steak)	5–6
Plaice (whole)	4–6
Plaice (fillet)	2–3
Salmon (steak)	5–6
Skate	5–6
Tuna (steak)	1–2

Times given for fish weighing approximately
175–225g (6–8oz).

Oven temperatures

°C	(fan)	°F	gas	description
110	(90)	225	¼	cool
120/130	(100/110)	250	½	cool
140	(120)	275	1	very low
150	(130)	300	2	very low
160/170	(140/150)	325	3	low to mod
180	(160)	350	4	moderate
190	(170)	375	5	moderately hot
200	(180)	400	6	hot
220	(200)	425	7	hot
230	(210)	450	8	hot
240 (	220)	475	9	very hot

Guide to recommended equivalent settings,
not exact conversions. Always refer to your cooker
instruction book.

Roasting times: meat

Set oven temperature to 180°C/350°F/Gas 4.

	cooking time per 450g/1lb	extra cooking time
Beef		
rare	20 min	20 min
medium	25 min	25 min
well done	30 min	30 min
Lamb		
medium	25 min	25 min
well done	30 min	30 min
Pork		
medium	30 min	30 min
well done	35 min	35 min

Let the cooked meat rest for 5–15 minutes before
carving to allow the juices to be reabsorbed and to
make carving easier

Steaming times: vegetables

	minutes
Asparagus	5–7
Beansprouts	3–4
Beetroot (sliced)	5–7
Broccoli (florets)	5–7
Brussels sprouts	5–7
Cabbage (chopped)	4–6
Carrots (thickly sliced)	5–7
Cauliflower (florets)	5–7
Courgettes (sliced)	3–5
Green beans	5–7
Leeks	5–8
Mangetout peas	3–5
Peas	3–5
Potatoes (cubed)	5–7

Times given are for steaming from when water has
started to boil.

Roasting times: poultry

	oven temperature	cooking time per 450g/1lb	extra cooking time	resting time
Chicken	200°C/400°F/Gas 6	20 min	30 min	15 min
Turkey (stuffed weight)				
small (under 6kg/13lb)	200°C/400°F/Gas 6	12 min	20 min	30 min
large	180°C/350°F/Gas 4	16 min	—	30 min
Duck	200°C/400°F/Gas 6	35 min	—	15 min
	for 45 min then 180°C/350°F/Gas 4			

* Note that for fan ovens, cooking times are generally reduced by 10 minutes for every hour.

Clever cooking

No matter how much spare cash we may or may not have, no one likes to throw away food. Not only is it wasteful but it's damaging to the environment too.

If we all stopped wasting the food that could be eaten, the benefit to the planet would be the equivalent of taking one in four cars off the road. Luckily, cutting food waste is easy!

Great cooking begins with an organised kitchen and proper planning. This doesn't negate the chance for spontaneous dishes, but reduces food waste and ensures that all the ingredients required are at hand.

Forward planning

Before you do your weekly shop, plan your meals for the next five days. Check your fridge or freezer first to see what you can make use of.

Browse your recipes and write your chosen meal down on a noticeboard or list on the fridge. Then write your shopping list based on these meals (plus any other foods that you need for breakfast, lunch and snacks).

When you have eaten the first five meals look at what you have left in your fridge, freezer and cupboard and create your final two meals from leftovers. Don't forget to include opened jars and packets as well as fresh foods. Be creative!

Clever storage

Place items in your fridge with the shortest shelf-life at the front. Keep fresh food in the packet it came in – some use clever technology to prolong their shelf life. Be freezer-friendly; check use-by dates and anything you are unlikely to use before its date pop in the freezer (check its label and don't freeze if it's already been frozen).

Seal open packets with pegs or decant into storage jars to prevent them from drying out.

If you cook too much, allow to cool, pop into a freezer-proof tub, label and freeze. This works especially well for meals such as stews and curries, where it makes sense to batch-cook. To defrost, place the tub in the fridge overnight, then heat until piping hot in the microwave or on the hob.

Whizz dry bread in a food processor, seal in bags and freeze. Grate ginger, chop herbs and chillies and store in ice cube trays in the freezer.

Savvy shopping

Try to stick to your list. If you are tempted by multibuy offers make sure that you freeze anything that you are unlikely to use before its use-by date. If you often throw away fruit and veg, buy them loose rather than in large packs.

If you have a small household you can buy small portions of meat and fish from the meat/fish counter or from your local butcher/fishmonger. If you want to bulk-buy (which can be more economical) split your pack of meat/fish into portions, wrap well and freeze.

Grow your own herbs on your windowsill or by the back door in summer. A plentiful supply of fresh herbs is so useful and much cheaper than buying from the supermarket.

Creative cooking

Try to use what you already have before buying new ingredients. This encourages your creativity as well as reducing food waste:

Create amazing salads using leftover leaves, veg, fruit and nuts or seeds. For leafy salads make dressings using oils and vinegars with herbs or mustards. For crunchy salads, creamy dressings work well, using crème fraîche or mayonnaise.

Stir leftover cold meat or fish into pasta with pesto, crème fraîche or fromage frais. Or add to an omelette with herbs, cheese and vegetables.

All sorts of veg can be used in an egg fried rice and leftover cured meats, such as chorizo or Parma ham are a brilliant addition too.

Vegetables which are slightly past their best can be cooked in stock and whizzed with a stick blender for soup, which freezes brilliantly.

And last but not least, use almost anything to top a baked potato. Sometimes, simple food can be the best!

Now, enjoy perusing your recipes for new ideas and shop with a clear conscience.

Grow your own fruit

Growing your own fruit can be exceptionally rewarding. Not only does the fruit you grow taste great but you have the added benefit of knowing exactly where it has come from and how it has been grown.

You can be sure that the fruit you eat is entirely organic and GM free. You do not need an enormous garden to grow fruit; even if you only have a small yard or balcony you can grow a fruit tree or plant in a pot.

Fruit that can be grown in containers

- Apples
- Blueberries
- Gooseberries
- Grapes
- Peaches
- Pears
- Plums
- Raspberries
- Redcurrants
- Strawberries

Getting started

It is advisable to obtain a few common gardening tools, including a spade, fork, hoe, rake, trowel, watering can and wheelbarrow. If you plan to grow fruit trees, secateurs, loppers and a small pruning saw are pretty essential.

When it comes to deciding what you will grow it really does depend on your taste. Choose fruit that you and your family or friends really enjoy. If you like to cook, why not try fruits that are suitable for jam making, tasty pies or scrumptious crumbles? You also need to ensure that there is a suitable place in your garden for the fruit variety you choose. If you plan to grow apples or pears, you will need to grow at least two different varieties (that flower at the same time) for pollination.

Fruit plants are available with bare roots or in pots. Both will work equally well, as long as you plant at the optimum time (see Planting calendar on page 26) and ensure that you plant them as soon as you have made your purchase. Organically grown fruit plants are now readily available. Look out for varieties that are pest and disease resistant for the best yield and most successful fruit. Before planting anything always read the instructions on the plant's label.

Planting

For fruit to thrive, the soil in which it is to be planted must be entirely free from weeds. Fork out any plants and weeds, and improve the soil quality with some compost or manure. Dig out planting holes a little larger than the root ball and gently place the plant in the ground.

Fill with soil and press down gently. For lower maintenance gardening, you may want to use a weed suppressant fabric around the plants. Space plants according to their instructions. Trees need to be supported with a short stake, and trained forms of fruit need canes, wires or posts to support them.

Maintenance

During the growing season check your fruit bushes and trees at least once a week. Remove any weeds within a metre or yard radius from the plant or tree. To do this you can use a hoe but always weed by hand when the soil is moist. To help prevent weeds from growing you can apply a mulch to the soil; during May, spread straw, leaves or rotted manure thickly around the plant over warm, wet soil. This mulch will help to retain moisture but even so, in dry hot weather you may need to water your plants each week. Check the soil just below the surface with your finger; if it feels dry then water with a watering can.

When checking your plants, pick off any pests and prune out any disease. To prune, always cut just above a bud, side shoot or branch. Never prune in frosty weather. Ensure plums are pruned between the end of May and early September. For autumn-fruiting raspberries cut all canes to the ground in winter, summer fruiting raspberries (old canes) should be cut immediately after fruiting. Trim old foliage and runners from strawberry plants after fruiting. Many top fruits set more fruit than they can ripen so it is a good idea to reduce the numbers by thinning. Keep the best fruit and remove the rest so there is about a 15cm (6in) gap between each fruit.

Where to plant

Decide what you want to grow, then choose your plot accordingly.

- For fruit to thrive it is best to choose a sunny spot and provide some shelter, such as a wall or fence.
- South facing walls are ideal for pears and plums.
- South-west or west facing areas are preferable for apples.
- North facing walls are ideal for redcurrants, gooseberries and some cooking apples.
- Strawberries and raspberries are usually grown in a row.
- Redcurrants and gooseberries can grow in rows or fans against a fence or wall.
- Apples, pears and plums can be planted as trees in a lawn or against a fence as fans.

Planting calendar

Fruit	Planting time	Notes
Apples	November	Plant to the same depth as in the pot
Apricots	October	Not suitable for frosty areas
Blackberries	October-November	Can be planted in shade
Blackcurrants	November	Plant 5cm (2in) deeper than in the pot
Blueberries	Spring, after frosts	Plant two varieties to ensure cross-pollination
Gooseberries	November	Plant bushes 1.2m (4ft) apart
Grapes	Winter	Plant just below the original compost surface
Peaches	October	Plant against a large south facing wall
Pears	November	Plant to the same depth as in the pot
Plums	October-early December	Choose variety according to the size of your garden
Raspberries	November	Plant 40cm (16in) apart, in rows
Redcurrants	November	Plant bushes 1.2m (4ft) apart
Strawberries	September	Plant 30cm (12in) apart, in rows

These may vary, depending on the variety; always read the plant instructions.

Dealing with disease and pests

If you can, try to deal with any problems you encounter using organic methods. This will ensure that the fruit you eat hasn't absorbed any chemicals.

Cover plants with netting to discourage birds. If you see any slugs pick off by hand and use traps. Squash aphids by hand and spray with insecticidal soap. Use sticky barriers to attract other insects.

If possible, try to buy disease-resistant plants. If you do experience problems, act swiftly and deal with the issue straight away. With brown rot, prune out any diseased wood and remove any windfall apples or plums. If you see canker, cut out all affected wood and burn the branches. Deal with apple and pear scab by cutting out any diseased twigs you see. If you discover cane spot or cane blight on your raspberries, cut out the diseased canes and burn them. To avoid crown rot in strawberries, never plant where strawberries have been grown before. Never water strawberries with grey mould, remove any infected foliage and fruit immediately. Deal with mildew by pruning out any affected shoots and fruits.

Uses for a glut of fruit

- Chop fruit into small pieces and add to salads.
- Make your own jelly or jam.
- Add pieces of fruit to curry to give a subtle sweet flavour.
- Try making fresh fruit cordial.
- For a drink, whizz with milk, yogurt or ice cream in a food processor.
- Make fruit pies or crumbles.

Websites

www.gardenaction.co.uk

www.gardenadvice.co.uk

www.rhs.org.uk

Stain removal

The most important factor in attacking stains is to act swiftly. The newer the stain, whether greasy or non-greasy, or a combination of the two, the easier it will be to remove without damage.

Personal

Blood: Soak in biological detergent and cold water, or cold water with salt added, and wash in heavy-duty biological detergent. Or try rubbing a mixture of cornflour and cold water into the stain, leaving to dry and brushing off.

Collar and cuff dirt: Apply liquid biological detergent directly with an old toothbrush. Wash as usual.

Deodorant: Sponge with a hydrogen peroxide solution (see box); apply heavy-duty liquid detergent to the area; wash.

Perspiration: Dab with white vinegar solution (see box); leave for 5 minutes. Soak and wash in biological detergent.

Urine and vomit: Soak in biological detergent and cold water, and wash in heavy-duty biological detergent.

Foodstuffs

Egg, milk and gravy: Soak in biological detergent and cold water, and wash in heavy-duty biological detergent.

Chewing gum: Freeze to make the gum brittle, using an ice cube inside a plastic bag; scrape it off, dab with methylated spirits (see box) and wash as usual.

Chocolate: Apply biological liquid detergent to the area; wash in heavy-duty detergent (containing bleach). On white items, soak in hydrogen peroxide solution (see box) and wash. Or soak in milk and wash in washing-up liquid; dab any remaining stain with white vinegar (see box), leave and wash as usual. Also good for coffee marks.

Oil/salad dressings: Sprinkle with cornflour to absorb grease, brush off, soak with washing-up liquid and then wash as normal.

Beverages

Tea, coffee, soft drinks: Soak in cool water, use a pre-wash treatment and wash in heavy-duty detergent (with bleach). Or use a hydrogen peroxide solution (see box) before washing.

Red wine: Mop up excess liquid and treat as for oil. Or cover stain with salt and leave for 30

What to do

■ Remove any solids with a blunt knife, and blot liquids with white kitchen paper.

■ Apply stain remover to a small, unseen area and wait 5–10 minutes. If the fabric reacts, seek dry-cleaning advice. Avoid treating delicate or expensive fabrics, or those that require dry-cleaning only.

■ Don't over-soak the fabric with a cleaning agent. To avoid making a ring mark, use a soft, absorbent cloth to apply the cleaning agent and work in a circular motion from the outside inwards. Dab, rather than rub, because rubbing can damage the fabric and it can also spread the stain.

Cleaning kit

Detergents
Biological and heavy-duty liquid detergents.

Eucalyptus oil
Available from essential oils section of major chemists.

Hydrogen peroxide
Ask your chemist for 20 volume strength. Mix 1 part to 6 parts water; soak item for 30 minutes or until the stain has cleared.

Lighter fluid
Apply neat with cotton wool.

Methylated spirits
Available from chemists. Apply with cotton-wool buds.

Pre-wash treatments
Some of these are formulated to treat a whole raft of common stains, some are more specific. Follow the instructions on the container.

White spirit
Dab neat on to grease stains.

White vinegar
Mix 15ml vinegar to 300ml water (3 tsp to ½ pint).

■ Chemical treatment may damage old or worn fabric.

■ Always test the fabric first in an inconspicuous area. If in doubt, take a stained garment to a dry-cleaner.

---

minutes. Sponge with a warm solution of biological detergent (with bleach), rinse with cold water and wash as normal. If the stain has dried, treat as for blood. On upholstery and carpets, blot with white kitchen paper. If it cannot be rinsed, spray with soda water, or white wine, then mop with kitchen paper.

White wine: Rinse with plenty of warm water, or treat as tea.

Grease, glue, wax, oil and tar

Oil, fat, grease and tar: Dab the area with eucalyptus oil; wash in water as hot as the fabric allows.

Glue: Try to remove glue before it sets; apply methylated spirits (see box) for natural fabrics, or lighter fluid for synthetic fabrics.

Wax crayons, cosmetics and shoe polish: Treat with white spirit (see box) to remove the wax stain. Apply a pre-wash

treatment and wash in heavy-duty detergent (with bleach).

Miscellaneous

Grass and mud: Dab on methylated spirits (see box) and rinse off with warm soapy water. Apply a pre-wash treatment and then wash in heavy-duty detergent (with bleach). For a new stain, try soaking in white vinegar (see box), or squeeze on some lemon juice.

Ink, ballpoint and felt tip: Dab stain with methylated spirits, and then wash. For washable ink,

soak in milk before laundering.

Mildew: Bleach white fabrics, or soak, then wash in heavy-duty detergent (with bleach).

Nail varnish: Mop up liquid, then with stain side facing down on kitchen paper, flush with nail polish remover (this is quite strong, and should not be used on some man-made fabrics – be sure to test first). Use methylated spirits (see box) to remove remaining nail-varnish colour.

Rust: Cover with salt, squeeze lemon juice over the salt and leave for about 1 hour; wash.

Safety note
Some of the cleaning agents you will need contain chemicals that are poisonous or flammable, so always read the label carefully and store them away from children. For safety, work in a well-ventilated area.

Websites
diynot.com

persil.co.uk

stainexpert.co.uk

Washing instructions

Nearly all fabrics are machine washable these days, and most washing machines handle them with care. Sort clothes and linens by colour and fabric type, and check labels.

Unless absolutely necessary, try to wash clothes at 30 degrees, as this uses less energy and is kinder to the environment. In any case, avoid washing an item at a higher temperature than recommended by the manufacturer, because this can cause it to shrink or change colour.

Every so often, run a higher temperature programme with the machine empty, to clean out greasy residues and kill off any bacteria.

Loading tips

■ Fill your washing machine loosely. Overloading not only adds to the number of creases that will need ironing out, but can damage your clothes and even your machine.

■ If you are washing woollens, this may mean washing just two or three items in one load.

Textile cycles

Check both the temperature, given by the figure in the tub, and the machine-action bar(s) under it. The temperature may be indicated by dots (six for 95°, four for 60°, two for 40° and one for 30°).

Maximum agitation. Cotton cycle
White cotton or linen articles without special finishes.

Maximum agitation. Cotton cycle
Cotton, linen or viscose articles without special finishes where colours are fast at 60°C.

Maximum agitation. Cotton cycle
Cotton, linen or viscose where colours are fast at 40°C but not at 60°C.

Medium agitation. Synthetic cycle
Acrylics, acetate or triacetate, including mixtures with wool, polyester and wool blends.

Minimum agitation. Wool cycle
Wool, including blankets, wool mixed with other fibres, and silk.

Gentle agitation. Delicates cycle
Silk, acetates and mixed synthetics not colourfast at 40°C.

Hand wash only
See garment label for further instructions.

Do not machine or hand wash

Washing process

Garments with labels showing the wash tub without the bar may be mixed with those that do, provided that they are washed at the lowest temperature shown and the gentlest setting of machine agitation to protect delicate items.

No bar
Normal – maximum machine action

1 bar
Medium – reduced machine action

2 bars
Minimum – lowest machine action

Washing symbols

Wash tub: Washing process

Triangle: Bleaching

iron: Ironing settings

Square: Drying methods

Circle: Dry cleaning

Dry-cleaning/bleaching

A circle shows the item may be dry-cleaned and the letter P or F indicates the cleaning fluids that may be used by your professional dry-cleaner.

May be dry-cleaned

Do not dry-clean

Bleach may be used

Do not use chlorine bleach

Do not bleach

Drying symbols

Check the label to see if garment can be tumble-dried; the label may advise using a reduced heat setting by putting a single dot within the circle. Two dots indicate a higher heat setting.

May be tumble-dried

Do not tumble-dry

Hang dry

Drip dry recommended

Dry flat

Ironing

■ The dots inside the iron indicate the temperature setting. One dot represents the coolest setting and three dots the hottest. The table (right) is a guide to the temperature to use for specific types of fabric.

■ You should always use the setting recommended by the manufacturer. For some materials the advice may be that you iron on the wrong side of the fabric only, so check the label.

■ To avoid creases, store your clothes in drawers and wardrobes loosely; don't pack them in.

Hot (3 dots)
Cotton, linen and viscose fabrics.

Warm (2 dots)
Polyester mixtures and wool.

Cool (1 dot)   Acrylic, nylon, acetate, triacetate and polyester.

Do not iron

Clean & fresh home

Very few of us enjoy cleaning the house but unfortunately it is something that has to be done. There are literally hundreds of products on the market which claim to clean better and brighter than others. But are they really necessary? Using too many chemicals in your home can damage your health, as well as your purse. These chemicals can be ingested and may also irritate your skin. Use some of these tips for a clean, fresh and healthy home.

General

Carpets: vacuum at least once a week. To deodorise carpets, sprinkle with a little bicarbonate of soda and then vacuum.

Furniture: dust with a slightly damp duster once a week or once a fortnight.

Remove dust from lampshades with a sticky roller (often used for removing lint from clothing) or masking-tape.

Curtains and cushions: vacuum once a month to remove dust and pet hair.

Pet hairs: to remove from furniture and stair carpets use a clean, dry, green kitchen scouring pad.

Windows: clean with a few sprays of white vinegar and water solution (1 part vinegar to 9 parts water) and then buff dry with a paper towel.

Glass vase stain: to remove a stain from the bottom of a glass vase, fill with water and add two Alka-Seltzer tablets. If the vase is dirty and you cannot reach the bottom simply fill with hot soapy water, add a teaspoon of dry rice or lentils and shake vigorously.

Water marks: to remove from wood, rub with a little mayonnaise and then wipe clean with a damp cloth.

Silver: polish with lemon juice and then buff to a shine with a soft clean cloth.

Bathroom

Bath and shower curtain: if your bath needs a thorough clean, fill it with warm water and add some biological washing powder. If you have one, pop your shower curtain in at the same time. Leave to soak for a couple of hours and then give the curtain and bath a rub and rinse. Both bath and shower curtain should be fresh and clean. Hang your curtain immediately to avoid creases.

Bathroom cleaner spray: in a spray bottle mix 1 part white vinegar with 1 part vodka and 2 parts water and add your favourite essential oils.

Each week clean the bath, sink, toilet and floor with the solution.

Taps: use an old toothbrush to clean the taps thoroughly and clean plugholes with an old bottle brush.

Toilet bowl: leave two denture tablets in the toilet overnight. Flush in the morning and the toilet bowl should sparkle.

Soap residue: remove soap from your bathroom tiles with a spray of white vinegar diluted with an equal amount of water and a few drops of essential oil, then polish with a cloth.

Toothbrush mugs: regularly wash in a bowl of hot water with washing-up liquid or, if you have one, in the dishwasher.

Mirrors: apply a tiny amount of shaving foam or methylated spirit to your mirror and polish with a soft cloth, it will gleam.

Fragrance: add a few drops of your favourite essential oil to the inside of the toilet tissue roll for a fresh fragrance.

Bedroom

Bedding: wash at 60°C to ensure all the mites are killed. Or add a few drops of eucalyptus oil, which is known to help eliminate dust mites.

Mattress protectors: wash once a month, pillows and duvets twice a year.

Mattress: vacuum regularly to remove dust mites.

Wardrobe: regularly 'spring-clean' and give anything you no longer wear to a charity shop.

Shoes: sprinkle a little bicarbonate of soda into smelly shoes and leave overnight. Don't forget to empty before wearing them though!

Kitchen

Dishes: wash dishes after each meal. Don't leave them to accumulate. Always wash the cleanest items first, such as glasses and mugs, followed by plates and cutlery and then finally cookware.

Tea and coffee stains: remove from mugs by adding equal amounts of salt and vinegar. Leave for a few minutes, remove with kitchen paper and then wash well.

Food residue: to remove stubborn food from baking trays and roasting tins sprinkle with biological washing powder and add hot water. Leave to soak then wash as usual.

Kettle: add a couple of denture tablets with some water and leave overnight. Rinse well and any lime-scale should have disappeared.

Cupboard doors: clean with a microfibre cloth and a spray of white vinegar diluted with an equal amount of water and a few drops of essential oil.

Floor: regularly sweep and mop with hot, soapy water.

Stainless steel: use a tiny amount of olive oil on a cloth to clean appliances and then polish to a shine with a microfibre cloth.

Fridge, hob, oven and splash-back: Clean with a solution of 4 tablespoons of bicarbonate of soda mised with 1 litre (1 ¾ pints) of warm water.

Drains: to clean and refresh, mix 3 heaped tablespoons of washing soda crystals with 4 litres (7 pints) of warm water. Pour this down the drain and follow with hot water.

If the drain is clogged pour 3 tablespoons of bicarbonate of soda down the plughole and then follow with 3 tablespoons of white vinegar. Leave for 5 minutes and then flush with plenty of hot water.

Cleaning kit

- Alka-Seltzer tablets
- Bicarbonate of soda
- Biological washing powder or detergent
- Concentrated washing-up liquid
- Denture tablets
- Essential oils (peppermint, lemon or eucalyptus)
- Lemon juice
- Olive oil
- Methylated spirit
- Spray bottles
- Washing soda crystals
- White vinegar
- Salt
- Microfibre cloths, cut-up old t-shirt cloths and scouring pads
- Mop, bucket, brush, dustpan, old toothbrushes and bottlebrush
- Vacuum cleaner
- Vodka

First aid kit

Be prepared! Ensure you have the right kit, should an accident or emergency occur. Your first aid kit should be locked and kept in a cool, dry place, out of reach of children.

- Medicines should be checked regularly to make sure they are within their use-by dates.
- It is also useful to keep a small first aid kit ready to hand in the car.
- Purchase a bag or container with good handles that will hold your first aid items.

Check list

Plasters, in a variety of different sizes and shapes	Sticky tape
Small, medium and large sterile gauze dressings	Digital thermometer
Two sterile eye dressings	Skin rash cream, such as hydrocortisone or calendula
Triangular bandages	Cream or spray to relieve insect bites and stings
Crêpe rolled bandages	Antiseptic cream
Safety pins	Painkillers such as paracetamol or ibuprofen
Disposable sterile gloves	Child-friendly painkillers (if applicable)
Tweezers	Antihistamine tablets
Scissors	Distilled water, for cleaning wounds
Alcohol-free cleansing wipes	Eye wash and eye bath

KITCHEN & HOME
DIARY
2016

December

Week 53

28 Monday

Bank Holiday, UK

Meal ideas

29 Tuesday

Meal ideas

30 Wednesday

Meal ideas

31 Thursday

New Year's Eve

Meal ideas

1 Friday January

New Year's Day
Bank Holiday, UK

Meal ideas

W	T	F	S	S	M	T	W	T	F	S	S	M	T	W	T
13	14	15	16	17	18	19	20	21	22	23	24	25	26	27	28

January
Week 53

Saturday 2
☾ Last Quarter

Meal ideas

Sunday 3

Meal ideas

What's in season in January?

Beetroot	Apples	Dover sole
Brussels sprouts	Pears	Gurnard
Cauliflowers	Rhubarb	Haddock
Celeriac		Halibut
Celery		Hake
Chicory	Duck	Langoustines
Horseradish	Guinea fowl	Lemon sole
Jerusalem artichokes	Hare	Lobsters
Kale	Mallard	Mackerel
Kohlrabi	Partridge	Mussels
Leeks		Oysters
Parsnips	Turkey	Red mullet
Potatoes (maincrop)	Venison	Scallops (queen)
Salsify		Sea bream
Shallots	Clams	Skate
Swedes	Cockles	Turbot
Turnips	Dab	Winkles

January
Week 1

4 Monday
Bank holiday, Scotland

Meal ideas

5 Tuesday

Meal ideas

6 Wednesday
Epiphany

Meal ideas

7 Thursday

Meal ideas

8 Friday

Meal ideas

Saturday 9

Meal ideas

Sunday 10
● New Moon

Meal ideas

Spiced Chicken & Noodle Soup

Sunflower oil 2 tbsp
Shallots 2, peeled and sliced
Celery sticks 2, chopped
Root ginger 5cm (2in) piece, peeled & chopped
Garlic 3 cloves, peeled and sliced
Red chilli ½-1, deseeded and chopped
Chinese Five Spice Stir Fry Paste 2 tsp
Skinless chicken breasts 3
Lemongrass 2 sticks
Chicken stock 2 litres (3½ pints)
Dried rice noodles 125g (4½oz)
Spring onions 6, trimmed and sliced
Pak choi 3, trimmed and sliced
Chopped coriander 2 tbsp

Time 1 hr   Serves 4-6
Calories 353 per portion
Fat 7g of which 1.1g is saturated

1 Heat oil in a pan and add shallots, celery, half the ginger, garlic and half the chilli. Stir in paste and cook for 1 minute, stirring. Add chicken and cook for 5 minutes, stirring occasionally. Add lemongrass, pour in stock, bring up to boil, then simmer for 30 minutes.
2 Meanwhile, soak noodles in boiling water for 3-5 minutes, then drain.
3 Remove chicken from stock and shred. Strain stock into a pan and heat with noodles, chicken, remaining ginger and chilli, onions, and pak choi. Cook for 5 minutes until pak choi is tender. Scatter with coriander.

39

January
Week 2

11 Monday

Meal ideas

12 Tuesday

Meal ideas

13 Wednesday

Meal ideas

14 Thursday

Meal ideas

15 Friday

Meal ideas

W	T	F	S	S	M	T	W	T	F	S	S	M	T	W	T
29	30	31	1	2	3	4	5	6	7	8	9	10	11	12	13

January
Week 2

Saturday **16**
) First Quarter

Meal ideas

Sunday **17**

Meal ideas

Cheese & Ham Soufflé

Fresh breadcrumbs 25g (1oz)

Butter 25g (1oz), plus extra for greasing

Plain flour 25g (1oz)

Milk 150ml (¼ pint)

Sweet or hot paprika ½ tsp

Eggs 4 large, separated

Cheddar cheese 110g (4oz) grated, plus extra for sprinkling

Parmesan cheese 25g (1oz) grated, plus extra for sprinkling

Snipped chives 3 tbsp

Ham 150g (5oz), cut into thin strips

Time 1 hour   Serves 3
Calories 560 per portion
Fat 38g of which 20g is saturated

1 Preheat oven to 190°C/375°F/Gas 5. Grease 900ml (1½ pint) soufflé dish, and sprinkle breadcrumbs over base and sides.

2 Melt butter in a pan, add flour, then milk and bring up to boil, stirring constantly. Season and add paprika. Allow to cool a little, then beat in egg yolks. Add cheeses, chives and ham.

3 Whisk egg whites until stiff but not dry, then gently fold into sauce. Pour soufflé mixture into dish and sprinkle extra cheeses over the top.

4 Place on a baking tray and bake for 35-45 minutes, until well-risen, golden brown, and feels very firm, yet springy. Serve immediately.

41

January
Week 3

18 Monday

Meal ideas

19 Tuesday

Meal ideas

20 Wednesday

Meal ideas

21 Thursday

Meal ideas

22 Friday

Meal ideas

Saturday 23

Meal ideas

Sunday 24

Septuagesima Sunday
○ Full Moon

Meal ideas

Caramel Custard Sauce

V

Caster sugar 200g (7oz)
Eggs 6 large, yolks only
Whole milk 600ml (1 pint)
Vanilla pod 5-7.5cm (2-3in)

Time 1 hour   Makes 1 pint
Calories 408 per ¼ pint
Fat 16g of which 6.5g is saturated

1 Line a large plate with non-stick paper or non-stick foil. To make caramel: pour 150ml (¼ pint) of cold water into a saucepan, add caster sugar and stir continuously over a moderate heat until every granule of sugar has dissolved, using a pastry brush to brush sides of the pan down frequently with hot water to prevent crystallisation.
2 When sugar is completely dissolved, bring syrup up to boil and boil until it turns a light golden brown, then immediately pour onto foil and cool until hard.
3 In a large heatproof bowl, whisk egg yolks and milk together.
4 Break caramel into small pieces and add to bowl with egg and milk with vanilla pod.
5 Place bowl over a pan of gently boiling water, making sure bowl does not touch the water. Stir continuously until custard thickens.
6 Strain sauce through a nylon sieve into a serving jug. Serve hot with puddings or pies, or cold poured over vanilla ice cream.

January
Week 4

M	T	W	T	F	S	S	M	T	W	T	F	S	S	M	T
25	**26**	**27**	**28**	**29**	**30**	**31**	1	2	3	4	5	6	7	8	9

25 Monday
Burns' Night

Meal ideas

26 Tuesday

Meal ideas

27 Wednesday

Meal ideas

28 Thursday

Meal ideas

29 Friday

Meal ideas

Saturday **30**

Meal ideas

Sunday **31**

Meal ideas

Duck 'n' Roots

Clear honey 2 tbsp
Chicken stock 300ml (½ pint)
Tomato purée 2 tbsp
Soy sauce 4 tbsp
Olive oil 2 tbsp
Potatoes 450g (1lb), peeled and thinly sliced
Duck breasts 4 large, approx. 900g (2lb), skinned and thinly sliced
Celeriac 225g (8oz) prepared weight, peeled and cut into thin strips
Carrots 2–3 large, peeled and cut into thin strips
Celery 3 large sticks, trimmed and thinly sliced
Spring onions 4 large, trimmed and sliced diagonally
Grated ginger 1–2 tbsp
Cooked rice to serve, optional

1 Put the first four ingredients into a small bowl and whisk together.
2 Heat oil in a wok or very large frying pan, add potatoes and stir-fry until just lightly browned. Add duck strips and stir-fry for 1–2 minutes.
3 Add other vegetables and ginger, and stir-fry for another 4–5 minutes. Add sauce, reduce heat and continue cooking until vegetables are cooked but still firm. Serve immediately with rice, if using.

Time 30 mins   Serves 4
Calories 450 per portion
Fat 9g of which 1.5g is saturated

45

February
Week 5

1 Monday
☾ Last Quarter

Meal ideas

---

2 Tuesday

Meal ideas

---

3 Wednesday

Meal ideas

---

4 Thursday

Meal ideas

---

5 Friday

Meal ideas

W	T	F	S	S	M	T	W	T	F	S	S	M	T	W	T
17	18	19	20	21	22	23	24	25	26	27	28	29	1	2	3

February
Week 5

Saturday 6
Accession of Queen Elizabeth II

Meal ideas

Sunday 7
Quinquagesima Sunday

Meal ideas

What's in season in February?

Brussels sprouts	Rhubarb	Halibut
Cauliflowers		Hake
Celeriac	Guinea fowl	Langoustines
Chicory	Hare	Lemon sole
Jerusalem artichokes	Partridge	Lobsters
Kale	Turkey	Mackerel
Kohlrabi	Venison	Mussels
Leeks		Oysters
Parsnips	Clams	Red mullet
Potatoes (maincrop)	Cockles	Salmon
Purple sprouting broccoli	Dab	Scallops (queen)
Salsify	Dover sole	Skate
Shallots	Gurnard	Turbot
Swedes	Haddock	Winkles
Turnips		

47

February

8 Monday
● New Moon

Meal ideas

9 Tuesday
Shrove Tuesday

Meal ideas

10 Wednesday
Ash Wednesday

Meal ideas

11 Thursday

Meal ideas

12 Friday

Meal ideas

W	T	F	S	S	M	T	W	T	F	S	S	M	T	W	T
24	25	26	27	28	29	1	2	3	4	5	6	7	8	9	10

February
Week 6

Saturday 13

Meal ideas

Sunday 14
Quadragesima Sunday

St Valentine's Day

Meal ideas

Swedish-Style Pancakes

V

Blueberries 300g (11oz)
Caster sugar 110g (4oz)
Plain flour 110g (4oz)
Baking powder ½ level tsp
Eggs 2 large, beaten
Butter 50g (2oz), melted and cooled
Buttermilk 284ml tub
Icing sugar for sifting

Time 45 mins   Makes 20
Calories 78 per pancake with berries
Fat 3g of which 1.5g is saturated

1 Place blueberries in a saucepan and add 90g (3½oz) sugar. Cover and heat gently, stirring occasionally, until juices flow and berries are just softened. Keep warm.
2 Sift remaining sugar, flour, baking powder and pinch of salt into a bowl. Pour eggs into a well in the centre, gradually whisking into flour, slowly adding butter and buttermilk.
3 Heat and lightly grease a heavy-based frying pan with butter. Drop tablespoonfuls of mixture into pan and cook for 2 minutes or until bubbles appear and pancakes are lightly browned underneath.
4 Turn pancakes over and cook other side for 1–2 minutes. Keep warm and repeat until all mixture has been used.
5 Serve with blueberries and dusted with icing sugar.

49

February

Week 7

15 Monday
❯ First Quarter

Meal ideas

16 Tuesday

Meal ideas

17 Wednesday

Meal ideas

18 Thursday

Meal ideas

19 Friday

Meal ideas

February
Week 7

Saturday **20**

Meal ideas

Sunday **21**

Meal ideas

Lemon Sole with a Crunchy Topping

Lemon sole fillets 2

Breadcrumbs 4 tbsp

Lemon 1, finely grated rind and juice

Butter knob, diced

New potatoes to serve, optional

Green salad to serve, optional

Lemon wedges to serve, optional

1 Preheat oven to 200°C/400°F/
Gas 6. Place lemon sole fillets in a
wide, shallow ovenproof dish.

2 Mix breadcrumbs with lemon
rind and juice and season with salt
and freshly ground black pepper.
Top fish with breadcrumb mixture.
Dot with butter and bake for
20 minutes, or until fish is cooked.

3 If using, serve with steamed new
potatoes tossed in butter, green
salad and lemon wedges.

Time 25 mins   Serves 2
Calories 265 per portion
Fat 11g of which 5.8g is saturated

February
Week 8

22 Monday
○ Full Moon

Meal ideas

23 Tuesday

Meal ideas

24 Wednesday

Meal ideas

25 Thursday

Meal ideas

26 Friday

Meal ideas

W	T	F	S	S	M	T	W	T	F	S	S	M	T	W	T
9	10	11	12	13	14	15	16	17	18	19	20	21	22	23	24

February
Week 8

Saturday **27**

Meal ideas

Sunday **28**

Meal ideas

Chocolate & Ginger Truffles

V

Dark chocolate 110g (4oz), broken into pieces
Trifle sponge cakes 4, rubbed through a sieve to make crumbs
Crystallised stem ginger 75g (3oz), drained if in syrup and finely chopped
Apricot jam 4 tbsp
Ground almonds 75g (3oz)
Chocolate mini sprinkles 70g tub
Petit fours cases 20

Time 30 mins plus chilling
Makes 20   Calories 99 per truffle
Fat 5g of which 1.5g is saturated

1 Put chocolate into a large bowl and microwave until melted, or place bowl in a pan of hot water and stir until melted.
2 Add cake crumbs, chopped ginger, jam and almonds and mix together well. Allow to cool, divide into 20 equal pieces, and roll each one into a smooth ball.
3 Spread chocolate sprinkles onto a plate and roll each truffle in the sprinkles until evenly coated. Place in petit fours cases and refrigerate until firm.

29 Monday

Meal ideas

1 Tuesday March

St David's Day
☾ Last Quarter

Meal ideas

2 Wednesday

Meal ideas

3 Thursday

Meal ideas

4 Friday

Meal ideas

Saturday **5**

Meal ideas

Sunday **6**

Mothering Sunday

Fourth Sunday in Lent

Meal ideas

What's in season March?

Cauliflowers	Dover sole
Kale	Gurnard
Leeks	Hake
Purple sprouting broccoli	Langoustines
Salsify	Lemon sole
Spinach	Lobsters
Spring onions	Mussels
Swedes	Oysters
	Red mullet
Rhubarb	Salmon
	Shrimps
Cockles	Whitebait
Dab	Winkles

March

Week 10

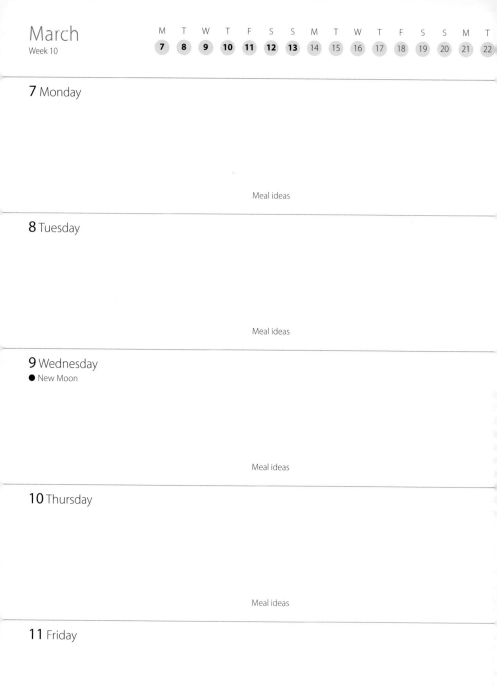

M	T	W	T	F	S	S	M	T	W	T	F	S	S	M	T
7	8	9	10	11	12	13	14	15	16	17	18	19	20	21	22

7 Monday

Meal ideas

8 Tuesday

Meal ideas

9 Wednesday

● New Moon

Meal ideas

10 Thursday

Meal ideas

11 Friday

Meal ideas

W	T	F	S	S	M	T	W	T	F	S	S	M	T	W	T
23	24	25	26	27	28	29	30	31	1	2	3	4	5	6	7

March
Week 10

Saturday **12**

Meal ideas

Sunday **13**

Meal ideas

Hollandaise Salmon

Butter 25g (1oz), melted
Salmon fillets 4
Lemon 1, sliced
Egg yolks 3
Caster sugar 1 tsp
White wine vinegar 1 tbsp
Lemon juice 1 tbsp
Butter 175g (6oz), diced
New potatoes, green beans and mangetout to serve, optional

1 Preheat oven to 150°C/300°F/ Gas 2. Brush 4 pieces of foil with melted butter and place a fillet on each. Add a lemon slice and season with freshly ground black pepper. Wrap loosely and bake for about 15 minutes, until cooked.
2 Meanwhile, make sauce by whisking egg yolks, sugar, vinegar and lemon juice with 1 tbsp water in a bowl set over a pan of simmering water, until mixture is smooth and leaves a trail on the surface.
3 Remove from heat and whisk in butter, a few pieces at a time. Season and pour into a jug. Serve salmon with warm sauce, new potatoes, steamed green beans and mangetout, if desired.

Time 25 mins   Serves 4
Calories 688 per portion
Fat 61.6g of which 30.5g is saturated

57

March
Week 11

---

14 Monday

Meal ideas

---

15 Tuesday
❭ First Quarter

Meal ideas

---

16 Wednesday

Meal ideas

---

17 Thursday
Bank Holiday, N Ireland
St Patrick's Day

Meal ideas

---

18 Friday

Meal ideas

W	T	F	S	S	M	T	W	T	F	S	S	M	T	W	T
30	31	1	2	3	4	5	6	7	8	9	10	11	12	13	14

March
Week 11

Saturday **19**

Meal ideas

Sunday **20**

Vernal equinox

Spring begins

Palm Sunday

Meal ideas

Colcannon with Bacon

Potatoes 680g (1½lb), peeled and chopped
Leek 1, trimmed and finely sliced
Savoy cabbage 225g (8oz), finely shredded
Milk 6 tbsp
Butter 40g (1½oz)
Nutmeg a pinch
Smoked back bacon rashers 8 slices

Time 30 mins   Serves 4
Calories 316 per portion
Fat 14g of which 7.4g is saturated

1 Cook potatoes in boiling water for 12–15 minutes until tender. Drain over another pan, so water can be used for cooking leek and cabbage. Bring water back up to boil, add greens and cook for 5 minutes.
2 Put potatoes back into first pan over a low heat to dry, then add milk, bring up to boil, remove from heat and add butter. Season with salt, pepper and nutmeg and mash until smooth.
3 Drain greens well and stir into mash.
4 Meanwhile, grill bacon for 3–5 minutes, until crisp. Cut into strips.
5 Divide mash between four bowls and pile bacon on top.

March
Week 12

21 Monday

Meal ideas

22 Tuesday

Meal ideas

23 Wednesday
○ Full Moon

Meal ideas

24 Thursday

Meal ideas

25 Friday

Bank Holiday, UK

Good Friday

Meal ideas

Saturday 26
Don't forget to put your clocks forward 1 hour tonight

Meal ideas

Sunday 27
British Summer Time begins

Easter Day

Meal ideas

Easter Cake

V ❄

Butter 350g (12oz)
Golden caster sugar 350g (12oz)
Eggs 6 large, beaten
Vanilla or almond essence 2 tsp
Self-raising flour 400g (14oz)
Finely ground hazelnuts 150g (5oz)
Ground almonds 150g (5oz)
Lemon curd 200g (7oz)
White marzipan 450g (1lb)
Clear honey 2 tbsp, warmed
Ready-to-roll fondant icing 1kg
(2lb 4oz)
Flowers and ribbon to decorate

1 Preheat oven to 160°C/325°F/Gas 3. Line
a 25cm (10in) round cake tin with baking
paper.
2 Beat butter and sugar together until
light and fluffy. Gradually beat in eggs, add
essence, then gently fold in flour and nuts.
3 Spoon mixture into tin, alternating with
spoonfuls of lemon curd. Smooth top. Bake
for 2 hours 20 minutes or until firm. Cool for
1 hour, then turn out onto a wire rack.
4 Roll out marzipan to cover top and sides
of cake. Brush cake with honey, cover with
marzipan, trim and smooth all over.
5 Roll out and cover cake with icing.
Decorate as per photo.

Time 3 hrs plus cooling
Serves 14   Calories 486 per slice
Fat 20.6g of which 7.5g is saturated

61

March

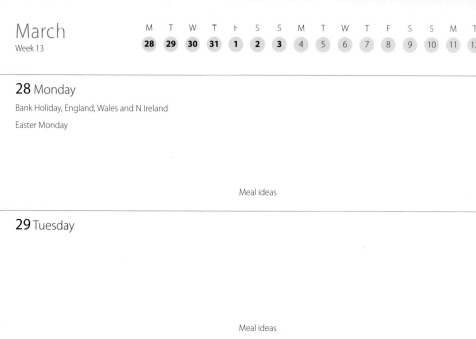

M T W T F S S M T W T F S S M T
28 29 30 31 1 2 3 4 5 6 7 8 9 10 11 12

28 Monday

Bank Holiday, England, Wales and N Ireland

Easter Monday

Meal ideas

29 Tuesday

Meal ideas

30 Wednesday

Meal ideas

31 Thursday

(Last Quarter

Meal ideas

1 Friday April

Meal ideas

Saturday **2**

Meal ideas

Sunday **3**
Low Sunday

Meal ideas

What's in season in April?

Asparagus	Rhubarb
Broccoli	Basil
Jersey Royal new potatoes	Chives
Lettuces	Dill
Purple sprouting broccoli	Sorrel
Radishes	
Rocket	Cockles
Salad leaves	Crab
Samphire	Langoustines
Spinach	Lobsters
Spring onions	Plaice
Watercress	Prawns
	Salmon
	Sea trout
Lamb	Shrimps
Wood pigeon	Whitebait

April
Week 14

4 Monday

Meal ideas

5 Tuesday

Meal ideas

6 Wednesday

Meal ideas

7 Thursday
● New Moon

Meal ideas

8 Friday

Meal ideas

W	T	F	S	S	M	T	W	T	F	S	S	M	T	W	T
20	21	22	23	24	25	26	27	28	29	30	31	1	2	3	4

April
Week 14

Saturday 9

Meal ideas

Sunday 10

Meal ideas

Savoury Muffins with Tomato & Chive Butter

Streaky bacon 175g (6oz), cut into thin strips
Fine cornmeal 110g (4oz)
Plain flour 175g (6oz)
Baking powder 1 tbsp
Snipped chives 3 tbsp
Butter 150g (5oz)
Eggs 2 large, beaten
Milk 225ml (8fl oz)
Sun-dried tomatoes 40g (1½oz), drained and chopped

1 Preheat oven to 220°C/425°F/ Gas 7. In a dry frying pan, gently fry bacon strips until lightly browned and crisp. Leave to cool. Line a muffin tray with muffin cases.
2 Sift cornmeal, flour and baking powder into a mixing bowl, mix in 2 tbsp chives and bacon, then make a well in centre.
3 Melt 75g (3oz) butter, mix with eggs and milk, then pour into flour. Mix gently, put into muffin cases and bake for 15–20 minutes until well risen, lightly browned and springy.
4 Blend remaining butter with tomatoes and remaining chives. Serve with warm muffins.

Time 30 mins   Makes 8
Calories 351 per portion
Fat 22g of which 11.7g is saturated

65

April
Week 15

11 Monday

Meal ideas

12 Tuesday

Meal ideas

13 Wednesday

Meal ideas

14 Thursday
❭ First Quarter

Meal ideas

15 Friday

Meal ideas

Saturday **16**

Meal ideas

Sunday **17**

Meal ideas

Pepper & Potato Salad

New potatoes 500g (1lb 2oz), scrubbed
Peppers 3 (1green, 1 red and 1 yellow)
Olive oil 6 tbsp
Red wine vinegar 2 tbsp
Lemon 1, finely grated rind & juice
English mustard ½ tsp
Chopped parsley 6 tbsp
Anchovy fillets in olive oil 200g can, drained
Red onion 1, peeled and thinly sliced into rings
Black olives 16

Time 30 mins plus standing
Serves 4   Calories 339 per portion
Fat 22g of which 3g is saturated

1 Cook potatoes in gently boiling, water until tender. Drain and cool.
2 Meanwhile, cook peppers under a hot grill until browned, turning frequently. Cool, then de-seed, peel and cut into thin strips. Keep juices.
3 Place olive oil, vinegar, lemon rind and juice, mustard and parsley in a salad bowl. Add reserved pepper juices. Whisk and season with salt and freshly ground black pepper.
4 Cut potatoes into thick slices and add to bowl with pepper strips, anchovies, onion rings and olives. Toss gently together. Leave to stand for 10–15 minutes before serving.

67

April
Week 16

M	T	W	T	F	S	S	M	T	W	T	F	S	S	M	T
18	**19**	**20**	**21**	**22**	**23**	**24**	25	26	27	28	29	30	1	2	3

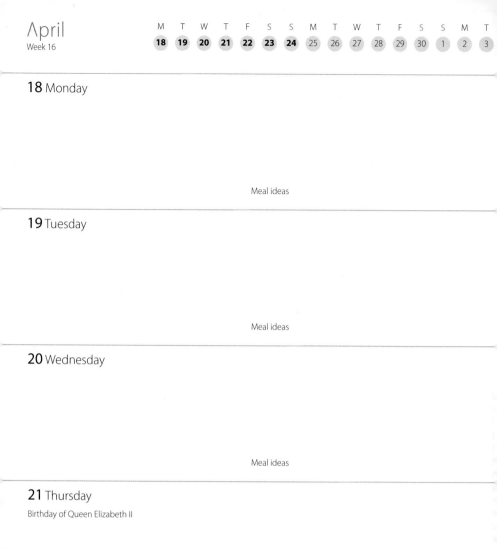

18 Monday

Meal ideas

19 Tuesday

Meal ideas

20 Wednesday

Meal ideas

21 Thursday

Birthday of Queen Elizabeth II

Meal ideas

22 Friday

○ Full Moon

Meal ideas

Saturday 23
St George's Day

Meal ideas

Sunday 24

Meal ideas

Steak & Mushroom Crumble ❄

Butter 75g (3oz)
Onion 1, peeled and chopped
Lean braising steak 450g (1lb), cubed
Plain flour 110g (4oz), plus 1 tbsp
Beef stock 600ml (1 pint)
Bay leaf 1
Wholegrain mustard 2 tsp
Button mushrooms 225g (8oz), wiped and sliced
Cheddar cheese 110g (4oz), grated
Chopped parsley 1 tbsp
Carrots with parsley to serve, optional

Time 2½ hours   Serves 4
Calories 537 per portion
Fat 33g of which 18.5g is saturated

1 Heat 25g (1oz) butter in a pan, add onion and fry for 3-4 minutes until softened. Toss steak in 1 tbsp of flour and add to pan. Cook for 5 minutes until browned all over.
2 Add stock, bay leaf and mustard, bring to boil, cover and cook for 1½ hours. Stir occasionally. Add mushrooms and cook for 10 minutes.
3 Rub remaining butter and flour together. Stir in cheese and parsley.
4 Discard bay leaf, place meat, onion, mushrooms and a little gravy into an ovenproof dish. Top with crumble mixture and bake at 200°C/400°F/Gas 6 for 30 minutes. Serve with remaining gravy and steamed carrots sprinkled with chopped parsley, if desired.

69

April
Week 17

25 Monday

Meal ideas

26 Tuesday

Meal ideas

27 Wednesday

Meal ideas

28 Thursday

Meal ideas

29 Friday

Meal ideas

W	T	F	S	S	M	T	W	T	F	S	S	M	T	W	T
11	12	13	14	15	16	17	18	19	20	21	22	23	24	25	26

April
Week 17

Saturday **30**
☾ Last Quarter

Meal ideas

May **Sunday 1**
Rogation Sunday

Meal ideas

What's in season in May?

Asparagus	Basil	Lamb
Broccoli	Chervil	Wood pigeon
Carrots	Chives	
Jersey Royal new potatoes	Coriander	Cod
Lettuces		Coley
New potatoes	Dill	Crab
Peas	Oregano	Haddock
Radishes		Langoustines
Rocket	Mint	Plaice
Salad leaves	Nasturtiums	Prawns
Samphire	Parsley (curly)	Salmon
Spinach		Sardines
Spring onions	Rosemary	Sea trout
Watercress	Sage	Shrimps
	Sorrel	Whelks
Rhubarb	Tarragon	Whitebait

May
Week 18

M	T	W	T	F	S	S	M	T	W	T	F	S	S	M	T
2	3	4	5	6	7	8	9	10	11	12	13	14	15	16	17

2 Monday
Bank Holiday, UK

Meal ideas

3 Tuesday

Meal ideas

4 Wednesday

Meal ideas

5 Thursday
Ascension Day

Meal ideas

6 Friday
● New Moon

Meal ideas

Saturday 7

Meal ideas

Sunday 8

Meal ideas

Coconut Prawns

Sesame oil 1 tbsp
Red onion 1, peeled and finely chopped
Cooked king prawns 350g (12oz), defrosted if frozen
Garlic 2 cloves, peeled and crushed
Frozen peas 75g (3oz)
Coconut cream 90ml (3fl oz)
Soy sauce 1 tbsp
Lime 1, finely grated rind and juice
Hot pepper sauce ½ tsp
Cooked rice to serve, optional
Chopped coriander 2 tbsp, optional

Time 10 mins   Serves 4
Calories 216 per portion
Fat 12g of which 7.3g is saturated

1 Heat oil in a wok and add onion, prawns, garlic, peas, coconut cream, soy sauce, lime zest and juice and pepper sauce. Stir-fry on a hot heat for about 4 minutes.
2 Serve on a bed of rice sprinkled with coriander, if using.

73

May
Week 19

9 Monday

Meal ideas

10 Tuesday

Meal ideas

11 Wednesday

Meal ideas

12 Thursday

Meal ideas

13 Friday
〉 First Quarter

Meal ideas

Saturday 14

Meal ideas

Sunday 15

Whit Sunday

Pentecost

Meal ideas

Pigs in Blankets

Medium-sliced white bread 8 slices
Butter 110g (4oz)
Tomato ketchup 3 tbsp
Wholegrain mustard 1 tbsp
Chopped parsley 4 tbsp
Thin pork sausages 8, skins removed
Cocktail sticks 16

1 Preheat oven to 220°C/425°F/ Gas 7. Cut crusts off each slice of bread, then roll each slice out with a rolling pin, to make thinner.
2 In a small saucepan, gently heat butter and ketchup until melted, then stir in mustard and parsley.
3 Brush butter mixture over one side of each slice of bread, then place a sausage diagonally across each one. Bring opposite corners up and over sausages to meet in centre, and secure with cocktail sticks.
4 Place wrapped sausages on a baking tray, brush with remaining butter mixture and bake in centre of oven for 25–30 minutes, until sausages are cooked and bread is lightly browned.

Time 40 mins   Makes 8
Calories 335 per portion
Fat 23g of which 11.4g is saturated

75

May
Week 20

16 Monday

Meal ideas

17 Tuesday

Meal ideas

18 Wednesday

Meal ideas

19 Thursday

Meal ideas

20 Friday

Meal ideas

W	T	F	S	S	M	T	W	T	F	S	S	M	T	W	T
1	2	3	4	5	6	7	8	9	10	11	12	13	14	15	16

May
Week 20

Saturday **21**
○ Full Moon

Meal ideas

Sunday **22**
Trinity Sunday

Meal ideas

Crème Fraîche Loaf

V ❄

Easy blend yeast 1 sachet
Strong white bread flour 225g (8oz)
Mixed spice 1 tsp
Caster sugar 5 tsp
Dried mango 75g (3oz), finely chopped
Raisins 50g (2oz)
Sultanas 50g (2oz)
Egg 1 large
Crème fraîche 2 tbsp
Melted butter 2 tbsp
Milk 2-3 tbsp

Time 50 mins plus proving
Makes 8 slices   Calories 225 per slice
Fat 6g of which 3.3g is saturated

1 Mix yeast, flour, spice, 3 tsp sugar, dried fruit and a pinch of salt. Crack in egg, add crème fraîche and butter, then mix to form a dough. Add 1 tbsp milk if dry.
2 Knead for 5 minutes. Return to bowl and cover. Leave in a warm place for about 30 minutes, until doubled in size.
3 Knead again for 5 minutes, then place in a greased 450g (1lb) loaf tin. Leave to rise again.
4 Preheat oven to 220°C/425°F/Gas 7. Bake for 10 minutes, reduce to 180°C/350°F/Gas 4, cover with foil and cook for 20–25 minutes until loaf sounds hollow when tapped. Glaze with 2 tsp sugar mixed with 2 tbsp warm milk and remove from tin.

May
Week 21

M	T	W	T	F	S	S	M	T	W	T	F	S	S	M	T
23	24	25	26	27	28	29	30	31	1	2	3	4	5	6	7

23 Monday

Meal ideas

24 Tuesday

Meal ideas

25 Wednesday

Meal ideas

26 Thursday

Corpus Christi

Meal ideas

27 Friday

Meal ideas

W	T	F	S	S	M	T	W	T	F	S	S	M	T	W	T
8	9	10	11	12	13	14	15	16	17	18	19	20	21	22	23

May
Week 21

Saturday 28

Meal ideas

Sunday 29
☾ Last Quarter

Meal ideas

Asparagus & Stilton Risotto V

Butter 25g (1oz)
Shallots 4, peeled and finely chopped
Garlic 1 clove, peeled and crushed
Risotto rice 300g (11oz)
White wine 150ml (¼ pint)
Hot vegetable stock 900ml (1½ pints)
Small asparagus spears 125g pack, trimmed
Frozen peas 110g (4oz)
Chopped parsley 2 tbsp
Stilton cheese 150g (5oz), cubed

Time 40 mins   Serves 4
Calories 518 per portion
Fat 20g of which 11.9g is saturated

1 Melt butter in a sauté pan and fry shallots and garlic for 3–4 minutes until softened. Stir in rice and fry for a further minute. Pour in wine and simmer until absorbed.
2 Gradually stir in hot stock, a ladleful at a time, for around 20 minutes, until rice is tender, and all stock has been absorbed. Add asparagus and peas for the last 5 minutes of cooking.
3 Before serving, stir in parsley and half the cheese, then season to taste. Spoon into bowls, scatter with remaining cheese and serve immediately.

30 Monday

Bank Holiday, UK

Meal ideas

31 Tuesday

Meal ideas

1 Wednesday June

Meal ideas

2 Thursday

Coronation Day

Meal ideas

3 Friday

Meal ideas

W	T	F	S	S	M	T	W	T	F	S	S	M	T	W	T
15	16	17	18	19	20	21	22	23	24	25	26	27	28	29	30

June
Week 22

Saturday **4**

Meal ideas

Sunday **5**
● New Moon

Meal ideas

What's in season in June?

Artichokes	Peas	Basil	Cod
Asparagus	Radishes	Chervil	Coley
Aubergines	Rocket	Chives	Crab
Beetroot	Runner beans	Coriander	Haddock
Broad beans	Salad leaves	Dill	Halibut
Broccoli	Samphire	Elderflowers	Herrings
Carrots	Spinach	Oregano	Langoustines
Chillies	Spring onions	Mint	Plaice
Courgettes	Tomatoes	Nasturtiums	Pollack
Fennel	Turnips	Parsley (curly)	Prawns
French beans	Watercress	Parsley (flat-leafed)	Salmon
Garlic		Rosemary	Sardines
Jersey Royal new		Sage	Scallops (queen)
potatoes	Bilberries	Sorrel	Sea bream
Kohlrabi	Blueberries	Tarragon	Sea trout
Lettuces	Cherries	Thyme	Shrimps
Mangetout	Gooseberries		Squid
New potatoes	Greengages	Lamb	Whelks
Onions	Strawberries	Wood pigeon	Whitebait
Pak choi			

June
Week 23

M	T	W	T	F	S	S	M	T	W	T	F	S	S	M	T
6	7	8	9	10	11	12	13	14	15	16	17	18	19	20	21

6 Monday
Bank Holiday

Meal ideas

7 Tuesday

Meal ideas

8 Wednesday

Meal ideas

9 Thursday

Meal ideas

10 Friday
Birthday of Duke of Edinburgh

Meal ideas

Saturday **11**

Meal ideas

Sunday **12**
❭ First Quarter

Meal ideas

Summer Berry Milkshakes   **V**

Raspberries 110g (4oz)
Strawberries 150g (5oz), hulled
Vanilla ice cream 3 scoops
Whole milk 600ml (1 pint), chilled
Natural yogurt 150g (5oz)

1 Put all ingredients into a blender
and blend until smooth.
2 Pour milkshake through a sieve
into a large jug, and then pour into
four large, well-chilled glasses. Serve
immediately.

Time 10 mins   Makes 3
Calories 245 per portion
Fat 13g of which 8.1g is saturated

83

June
Week 24

M	T	W	T	F	S	S	M	T	W	T	F	S	S	M	T
13	**14**	**15**	**16**	**17**	**18**	**19**	20	21	22	23	24	25	26	27	28

13 Monday

Meal ideas

14 Tuesday

Meal ideas

15 Wednesday

Meal ideas

16 Thursday

Meal ideas

17 Friday

Meal ideas

W	T	F	S	S	M	T	W	T	F	S	S	M	T	W	T
29	30	1	2	3	4	5	6	7	8	9	10	11	12	13	14

June
Week 24

Saturday **18**

Meal ideas

Sunday **19**
Father's Day

Meal ideas

Lamb Shanks with Apricots

❄

Olive oil 1 tbsp
Butter 25g (1oz)
Lamb shanks 4
Onion 1, peeled and sliced
Plain flour 2 tbsp
Mixed ground spice 2 tsp
Oranges 2 large, pared rind and juice
Lamb or chicken stock 300ml (½ pint)
Dried apricots 250g (9oz)
Herby couscous to serve, optional

Time 2¼ hrs   Serves 4
Calories 952 per portion
Fat 52g of which 25.2g is saturated

1 Preheat oven to 180°C/350°F/Gas 4. In a large flameproof casserole dish, heat olive oil and butter until sizzling. Then add lamb shanks and cook for about 2 minutes each side, until browned. Remove from casserole and set aside. Fry onion until just golden.
2 Stir flour and spice into casserole and add orange rind and juice and stock.
3 Bring to boil, stirring, and then return lamb shanks and coat well with liquid.
4 Add apricots and season. Cover with greaseproof paper to stop excess evaporation, cover with a lid and cook for 2 hours, turning over lamb after 1 hour. Serve on bed of couscous, if using.

85

June
Week 25

20 Monday

Summer solstice

Summer begins

○ Full Moon

Meal ideas

21 Tuesday

Meal ideas

22 Wednesday

Meal ideas

23 Thursday

Meal ideas

24 Friday

Meal ideas

W	T	F	S	S	M	T	W	T	F	S	S	M	T	W	T
6	7	8	9	10	11	12	13	14	15	16	17	18	19	20	21

June
Week 25

Saturday 25

Meal ideas

Sunday 26

Meal ideas

Coffee Battenberg

V

Butter 175g (6oz)
Caster sugar 175g (6oz)
Eggs 3, beaten
Self-raising flour 175g (6oz)
Coffee essence 4 tsp
Milk 1 tbsp
Ginger marmalade 10 tbsp
Marzipan 450g (1lb)
Crystallised ginger 2 pieces, chopped

1 Preheat oven to 180°C/350°F/Gas 4. Grease a 20cm (8in) square cake tin. Line with foil, making a pleat in centre to height of tin to divide in half, thengrease.
2 Beat butter and sugar together until light then beat in the eggs and flour alternately until smooth. Divide mixture in half, then fold coffee essence into one half and milk into other half.
3 Spoon one flavour into either side of tin. Bake for 30-35 minutes then turn onto a wire rack to cool.
4 Trim cakes to same size and cut both in half lengthways. Spread two sides of each with marmalade and gently push together. Roll out marzipan on non-stick baking paper dusted with icing sugar until large enough to wrap around cake. Spread with marmalade and roll around cake. Trim off excess, crimp along edges. Decorate with ginger.

Time 1 hour   Serves 6-8
Calories 633 per slice
Fat 28g of which 12.7g is saturated

June

Week 26

M	T	W	T	F	S	S	M	T	W	T	F	S	S	M	T
27	28	29	30	1	2	3	4	5	6	7	8	9	10	11	12

27 Monday
☾ Last Quarter

Meal ideas

28 Tuesday

Meal ideas

29 Wednesday

Meal ideas

30 Thursday

Meal ideas

1 Friday July

Meal ideas

Saturday **2**

Meal ideas

Sunday **3**

Meal ideas

What's in season in July?

Artichokes	Radishes	Chives	Coley
Aubergines	Rocket	Coriander	Crab
Beetroot	Runner beans	Dill	Dover sole
Broad beans	Salad leaves	Elderflowers	Haddock
Broccoli	Samphire	Oregano	Halibut
Carrots	Spinach	Mint	Herrings
Chillies	Spring onions	Nasturtiums	Langoustines
Courgettes	Tomatoes	Parsley (curly)	Mackerel
Fennel	Turnips	Parsley (flat-leafed)	Plaice
French beans	Watercress	Rosemary	Pollack
Garlic		Sage	Prawns
Jersey Royal new	Bilberries	Sorrel	Salmon
potatoes	Blueberries	Tarragon	Sardines
Kohlrabi	Cherries	Thyme	Scallops (queen)
Lettuces	Gooseberries		Sea bream
Mangetout	Greengages	Lamb	Sea trout
New potatoes	Strawberries	Rabbit	Shrimps
Onions		Wood pigeon	Squid
Pak choi	Basil		Whelks
Peas	Chervil	Cod	Whitebait

July
Week 27

M	T	W	T	F	S	S	M	T	W	T	F	S	S	M	T
4	5	6	7	8	9	10	11	12	13	14	15	16	17	18	19

4 Monday
● New Moon

Meal ideas

5 Tuesday

Meal ideas

6 Wednesday

Meal ideas

7 Thursday

Meal ideas

8 Friday

Meal ideas

Saturday **9**

Meal ideas

Sunday **10**

Meal ideas

Maple Pecan Chicken

Garlic 1 clove, peeled and crushed
White wine vinegar 1 tbsp
Maple syrup 3 tbsp
Wholegrain mustard 2 tsp
Chopped pecan nuts 2 tbsp
Chicken thighs 4, skinned
Chips and salad to serve

1 In a large bowl mix garlic, vinegar,
maple syrup, mustard and chopped
nuts together.
2 Add chicken to bowl and coat in
sauce. Cover and chill overnight.
3 Preheat oven to 200°C/400°F/
Gas 6. Remove thighs from sauce,
spoon nuts and sauce on top and
bake on a tray lined with foil for
30 minutes, or until cooked through.
Serve with chips and salad.

Time 35 mins plus chilling
Serves 2   Calories 331 per portion
Fat 13g of which 2.5g is saturated

July
Week 28

M	T	W	T	F	S	S	M	T	W	T	F	S	S	M	T
11	12	13	14	15	16	17	18	19	20	21	22	23	24	25	26

11 Monday

Meal ideas

12 Tuesday

Bank Holiday, N Ireland
❯ First Quarter

Meal ideas

13 Wednesday

Meal ideas

14 Thursday

Meal ideas

15 Friday

Meal ideas

92

Saturday 16

Meal ideas

Sunday 17

Meal ideas

Pickled Beetroot   V

Fresh, uncooked beetroot 1.25–1.5kg (2½–3lb)
Cinnamon 5cm (2in) piece
Mace 3 pieces
Whole allspice 1 tsp
Whole peppercorns 1 tsp
Large dried chillies 3
Whole cloves 5
Caster sugar 2 tbsp
Distilled malt vinegar 5% acidity 700ml (1¼ pints)

Time 2 hours plus cooling
Makes 1.25–1.5kg (2½–3lb)
Calories 13 per 25g (1oz) Fat 0g

1 Wash beetroot and cut off stalks to within 2.5cm (1in) of each beetroot. Place beetroot in a large saucepan, cover with cold water and bring to boil. Reduce heat, cover and cook gently for 1–1½ hours until cooked. Drain and leave to cool overnight.
2 Meanwhile, place all spices in a saucepan, add sugar and 300ml (½ pint) vinegar and bring to boil. Remove from heat, cover and leave to cool overnight.
3 Peel cooked beetroot and cut into slices. Layer in clean jars.
4 Stir remaining vinegar into spiced vinegar, then pour into jars with spices, making sure beetroot is covered. Seal with lids and store in a cool, dry place.

July
Week 29

M	T	W	T	F	S	S	M	T	W	T	F	S	S	M	T
18	**19**	**20**	**21**	**22**	**23**	**24**	25	26	27	28	29	30	31	1	2

18 Monday

Meal ideas

19 Tuesday
○ Full Moon

Meal ideas

20 Wednesday

Meal ideas

21 Thursday

Meal ideas

22 Friday

Meal ideas

Saturday **23**

Meal ideas

Sunday **24**

Meal ideas

Gooseberry & Hazelnut Fool   V

Gooseberries 450g (1lb), trimmed
Caster sugar 65g (2½oz)
Custard powder 1 tbsp
Milk 300ml (½ pint)
Hazelnut yogurt 150g (5oz)
Hazelnuts 2 tbsp, chopped
Shortbread biscuits to serve, optional

1 Cook gooseberries with 50g (2oz)
sugar and 2 tbsp water for
20 minutes until soft. Purée.
2 Meanwhile, blend custard powder
with remaining sugar and 2 tbsp
milk. Bring remaining milk up to boil
then pour onto blended custard
powder. Return to pan and heat,
stirring, until custard boils and
thickens. Allow to cool completely.
3 Mix custard, gooseberry purée and
yogurt together. Spoon into serving
dishes and sprinkle with hazelnuts.
Serve with shortbread, if using.

Time 30 mins plus cooling
Serves 4   Calories 237 per portion
Fat 9g of which 3.3g is saturated

95

M	T	W	T	F	S	S	M	T	W	T	F	S	S	M	T
25	26	27	28	29	30	31	1	2	3	4	5	6	7	8	9

25 Monday

Meal ideas

26 Tuesday

☾ Last Quarter

Meal ideas

27 Wednesday

Meal ideas

28 Thursday

Meal ideas

29 Friday

Meal ideas

Saturday **30**

Meal ideas

Sunday **31**

Meal ideas

Fruity Chicken Salad

Lime 1, finely grated rind and juice
Garlic 1 clove, peeled and crushed
Green chilli 1, deseeded and finely chopped
Demerara sugar 40g (1½oz)
Soy sauce 1 tbsp
Skinless chicken breast 450g (1lb), thinly sliced
Olive oil 1 tbsp
Mixed salad leaves 200g (7oz)
Mango 1, peeled and cubed
Figs 4, quartered
Pistachio nuts 25g (1oz)

Time 20 mins plus marinating
Serves 4   Calories 295 per portion
Fat 8g of which 1.3g is saturated

1 For marinade, combine lime rind and juice, garlic, chilli, sugar and soy sauce. Pour over chicken, cover and chill for 2 hours.
2 Heat oil in a wok or frying pan. Add chicken and marinade and stir-fry for 8 minutes or until chicken is cooked through.
3 Place salad in serving bowls, then spoon on chicken, fruit and nuts. Serve immediately.

97

August
Week 31

M	T	W	T	F	S	S	M	T	W	T	F	S	S	M	T
1	**2**	**3**	**4**	**5**	**6**	**7**	8	9	10	11	12	13	14	15	16

1 Monday
Bank Holiday, Scotland

Meal ideas

2 Tuesday
● New Moon

Meal ideas

3 Wednesday

Meal ideas

4 Thursday

Meal ideas

5 Friday

Meal ideas

W	T	F	S	S	M	T	W	T	F	S	S	M	T	W	T
17	18	19	20	21	22	23	24	25	26	27	28	29	30	31	1

August
Week 31

Saturday 6

Meal ideas

Sunday 7

Meal ideas

What's in season in August?

Artichokes	Runner beans	Oregano	Halibut
Aubergines	Salad leaves	Mint	Herring
Beetroot	Spring onions	Parsley (curly)	Langoustines
Broad beans	Sweetcorn	Parsley (flat-leafed)	Lemon sole
Broccoli	Tomatoes	Rosemary	Mackerel
Carrots	Turnips	Sage	Monkfish
Chillies	Watercress	Sorrel	Pilchards
Courgettes	Wild mushrooms	Tarragon	Plaice
Cucumber		Thyme	Pollack
Fennel	Bilberries		Prawns
French beans	Blueberries	Beef	Red mullet
Garlic	Cherries	Lamb	Salmon
Kohlrabi	Damsons	Rabbit	Sardines
Lettuces	Greengages	Venison	Sea bass (wild)
Mangetout	Loganberries	Wood pigeon	Scallops (queen)
Marrows	Plums		Sea bass (wild)
Onions	Raspberries	Cod	Sea bream
Pak choi	Redcurrants	Coley	Sea trout
Peas	Strawberries	Crab	Shrimps
Peppers		Dab	Squid
Potatoes (maincrop)	Basil	Dover sole	Whelks
Radishes	Chives	Grey mullet	
Rocket	Coriander	Haddock	

August
Week 32

8 Monday

Meal ideas

9 Tuesday

Meal ideas

10 Wednesday
❭ First Quarter

Meal ideas

11 Thursday

Meal ideas

12 Friday

Meal ideas

W	T	F	S	S	M	T	W	T	F	S	S	M	T	W	T
24	25	26	27	28	29	30	31	1	2	3	4	5	6	7	8

August
Week 32

Saturday 13

Meal ideas

Sunday 14

Meal ideas

Red Pepper & Tomato Soup

V ❄

Red peppers 2 large
Olive oil 1 tbsp
Onion 1 large, peeled and chopped
Tomatoes 450g (1lb), chopped
Sun-dried tomato paste 2 tbsp
Vegetable stock 600ml (1 pint)
Dried oregano ½ tsp
Green pesto for drizzling, optional

Time 1 hr plus cooling
Serves 4   Calories 125 per portion
Fat 6g of which 0.5g is saturated

1 Preheat grill to high. Place peppers on rack in a grill pan and cook, turning frequently, until the skin is lightly charred all over. Put into a bowl, cover with cling film and cool.
2 Remove skin and seeds (reserve juices), then chop.
3 In a large saucepan, heat oil, add onion and cook until slightly softened, but not browned.
4 Add peppers, tomatoes, tomato paste, stock and oregano. Bring up to boil, then reduce the heat, cover and cook for 40–45 minutes until tomatoes are soft.
5 In batches, pour soup into a blender and blend until smooth. Season to taste and serve with a drizzle of pesto, if using.

101

August
Week 33

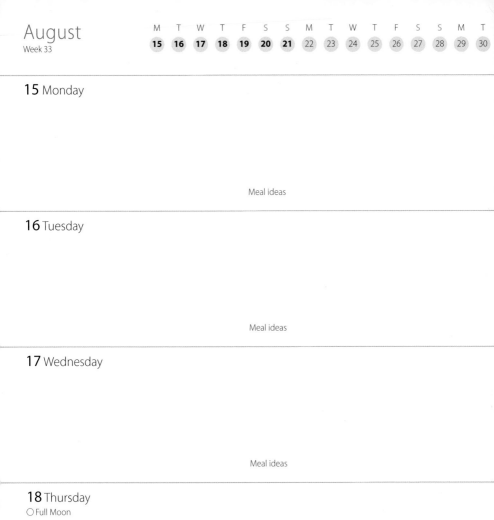

M **15** T **16** W **17** T **18** F **19** S **20** S **21** M 22 T 23 W 24 T 25 F 26 S 27 S 28 M 29 T 30

15 Monday

Meal ideas

16 Tuesday

Meal ideas

17 Wednesday

Meal ideas

18 Thursday
○ Full Moon

Meal ideas

19 Friday

Meal ideas

W | T | F | S | S | M | T | W | T | F | S | S | M | T | W | T
31 | 1 | 2 | 3 | 4 | 5 | 6 | 7 | 8 | 9 | 10 | 11 | 12 | 13 | 14 | 15

August
Week 33

Saturday 20

Meal ideas

Sunday 21

Meal ideas

Cherry & Spice Biscuits

V ❄

Butter 110g (4oz), softened
Caster sugar 75g (3oz), plus 1–2 tbsp
Egg 1, separated
Plain flour 200g (7oz)
Ground ginger ½ tsp
Ground cinnamon ½ tsp
Dried cherries 75g (3oz)

Time 30 mins   Makes 12 biscuits
Calories 183 per biscuit
Fat 8.4g of which 5g is saturated

1 Preheat oven to 200°C/400°F/ Gas 6. Grease a baking sheet.
2 Cream butter and sugar together in a bowl and beat in egg yolk. Sift in flour, ginger and cinnamon and gently fold into creamed mixture. Stir in cherries and shape mixture into a ball of dough.
3 Knead dough on a lightly floured surface and roll out to a 5mm (¼in) thickness. Use an 8cm (3¼in) cutter to cut out 12 biscuits. Place on baking sheet and bake in oven for 10 minutes.
4 Meanwhile, lightly beat egg white. Remove biscuits from oven and brush with egg white. Sprinkle with caster sugar and bake for a further 5 minutes until golden.

August
Week 34

22 Monday

Meal ideas

23 Tuesday

Meal ideas

24 Wednesday

Meal ideas

25 Thursday
☾ Last Quarter

Meal ideas

26 Friday

Meal ideas

W	T	F	S	S	M	T	W	T	F	S	S	M	T	W	T
7	8	9	10	11	12	13	14	15	16	17	18	19	20	21	22

August
Week 34

Saturday 27

Meal ideas

Sunday 28

Meal ideas

Easy Peanut Noodles

V

Sesame oil 1 tbsp
Courgette 1, cut into thin sticks
Carrots 2, peeled and cut into thin sticks
Baby corn 125g pack
Mushrooms 110g (4oz), wiped and sliced
Straight-to-wok noodles 300g pack
Milk 4 tbsp
Sweet chilli sauce 1 tbsp
Crunchy peanut butter 2 tbsp
Coriander to garnish, optional

1 Heat oil in a wok and stir-fry vegetables for about 5 minutes.
2 Add noodles to wok and warm through for 2 minutes.
3 Meanwhile, put milk, chilli sauce and peanut butter in a bowl and microwave on full power for 30–40 seconds. Whisk together.
4 Just before serving, stir peanut sauce into noodles and vegetables. Divide between two bowls and top with coriander leaves, if using.

Time 15 mins   Serves 2
Calories 474 per portion
Fat 17g of which 3.1g is saturated

105

August
Week 35

29 Monday
Bank Holiday, England, Wales and N Ireland

Meal ideas

30 Tuesday

Meal ideas

31 Wednesday

Meal ideas

1 Thursday September
● New Moon

Meal ideas

2 Friday

Meal ideas

W	T	F	S	S	M	T	W	T	F	S	S	M	T	W	T
14	15	16	17	18	19	20	21	22	23	24	25	26	27	28	29

September
Week 35

Saturday 3

Meal ideas

Sunday 4

Meal ideas

What's in season in September?

Artichokes	Radishes	Coriander	Crab
Aubergine	Rocket	Oregano	Dab
Beetroot	Runner beans	Mint	Dover sole
Broccoli	Salad leaves	Parsley (curly)	Grey mullet
Butternut squash	Shallots	Parsley (flat-leafed)	Haddock
Carrots	Spring onions	Rosemary	Halibut
Celeriac	Sweetcorn	Sage	Hake
Celery	Tomatoes	Sorrel	Herring
Chillies	Turnips	Thyme	Lemon sole
Courgettes	Watercress		Mackerel
Cucumber	Wild mushrooms	Beef	Monkfish
Fennel		Duck	Mussels
French beans	Apples	Grouse	Oysters
Garlic	Bilberries	Guinea fowl	Pilchards
Horseradish	Blackberries	Hare	Plaice
Kale	Damsons	Lamb	Pollack
Kohlrabi	Elderberries	Mallard	Prawns
Leeks	Pears	Pheasant	Red mullet
Lettuces	Plums	Rabbit	Sea bass (wild)
Mangetout	Raspberries	Turkey	Sea bream
Marrows	Redcurrants	Venison	Shrimps
Onions		Wood pigeon	Squid
Pak choi	Chestnuts		Turbot
Peppers	Cob nuts	Clams	Whelks
Potatoes (maincrop)		Cod	Winkles
Pumpkins	Chives	Coley	

107

September

M	T	W	T	F	S	S	M	T	W	T	F	S	S	M	T
5	**6**	**7**	**8**	**9**	**10**	**11**	12	13	14	15	16	17	18	19	20

5 Monday

Meal ideas

6 Tuesday

Meal ideas

7 Wednesday

Meal ideas

8 Thursday

Meal ideas

9 Friday
❯ First Quarter

Meal ideas

W	T	F	S	S	M	T	W	T	F	S	S	M	T	W	T
21	22	23	24	25	26	27	28	29	30	1	2	3	4	5	6

September
Week 36

Saturday 10

Meal ideas

Sunday 11

Meal ideas

Slow-Cooked Fruity Beef Curry

Plain yogurt 150g (5oz)
Garlic 1 clove, peeled and crushed
Curry powder 1 tbsp
Lean stewing beef 680g (1½lb), cubed
Milk 150ml (¼ pint)
Tomatoes 400g can
Beef stock 150ml (¼ pint)
Ready-to-eat dried tropical fruit 175g (6oz)
Cornflour 25g (1oz)
Steamed rice to serve, optional
Coriander to garnish, optional

Time 2¼ hours plus marinating
Serves 6   Calories 266 per portion
Fat 6g of which 2.5g is saturated

1 Blend yogurt, garlic and curry powder in a bowl and stir in beef. Leave to marinate for at least 1 hour.
2 Place beef and its marinade in a large pan. Add milk, tomatoes, stock and fruit. Cover, bring up to boil and simmer for 2 hours or until tender.
3 Blend cornflour with a little milk, stir into curry and heat until sauce thickens and boils. Cook for 1 minute then serve with steamed rice, if using, and garnish with coriander.

109

September
Week 37

12 Monday

Meal ideas

13 Tuesday

Meal ideas

14 Wednesday

Meal ideas

15 Thursday

Meal ideas

16 Friday
○ Full Moon

Meal ideas

W	T	F	S	S	M	T	W	T	F	S	S	M	T	W	T
28	29	30	1	2	3	4	5	6	7	8	9	10	11	12	13

September
Week 37

Saturday **17**

Meal ideas

Sunday **18**

Meal ideas

Sausage Goulash

Pork sausages 8
Onions 2 large, peeled, each cut into 6 lengthways
Garlic cloves 2–3, peeled and crushed
Green peppers 2, de-seeded and thickly sliced
Sweet paprika 1 tbsp
Plain flour 1 tbsp
Chicken stock 300ml (½ pint)
Chopped tomatoes 400g can
Soured cream, sliced pickled dill cucumbers and chopped parsley for serving, optional

1 Preheat oven to 180°C/350°F/Gas 4. Heat a large casserole and cook sausages until lightly browned. Remove and set aside.
2 Add onions, garlic and peppers and cook gently until slightly softened. Stir in paprika, flour, stock and tomatoes and bring to boil.
3 Return sausages to pan, coat well with sauce. Cover surface with greaseproof paper. Cover with lid, then cook in oven for 1–1¼ hours.
4 Skim off excess fat. Top with soured cream, pickled cucumbers, and parsley, if using.

Time 1½ hours   Serves 4
Calories 401 per portion
Fat 26g of which 8.3g is saturated

111

September
Week 38

19 Monday

Meal ideas

20 Tuesday

Meal ideas

21 Wednesday

Meal ideas

22 Thursday

Autumnal equinox

Autumn begins

Meal ideas

23 Friday

☾ Last Quarter

Meal ideas

W	T	F	S	S	M	T	W	T	F	S	S	M	T	W	T
5	6	7	8	9	10	11	12	13	14	15	16	17	18	19	20

September
Week 38

Saturday 24

Meal ideas

Sunday 25

Meal ideas

Cheese & Tomato Bake

V ❄

Sliced bread 4 slices, crusts removed
Butter 25g (1oz)
Tomatoes 2, sliced
Mature Cheddar cheese 75g (3oz), grated
Eggs 2
Milk 150ml (¼ pint)

1 Preheat oven to 200°C/400°F/ Gas 6 and place a baking sheet in oven to heat up.
2 Cut bread in half diagonally, spread with butter on one side and arrange, overlapping, in a small gratin dish. Insert tomato slices between bread and scatter with cheese, lifting up bread slices so that some cheese falls underneath.
3 Beat eggs with milk, then season and pour over bread.
4 Place dish on baking sheet and bake for about 25 minutes, until a light golden colour and firm. Serve immediately.

Time 30 mins   Serves 2
Calories 554 per portion
Fat 32.9g of which 1.5g is saturated

113

September
Week 39

M	T	W	T	F	S	S	M	T	W	T	F	S	S	M	T
26	27	28	29	30	1	2	3	4	5	6	7	8	9	10	11

26 Monday

Meal ideas

27 Tuesday

Meal ideas

28 Wednesday

Meal ideas

29 Thursday

Meal ideas

30 Friday

Meal ideas

October **Saturday 1**
● New Moon

Meal ideas

Sunday 2

Meal ideas

What's in season in October?

Artichokes	Shallots	Beef	Gurnard
Beetroot	Swedes	Duck	Haddock
Broccoli	Sweetcorn	Goose	Halibut
Butternut squash	Tomatoes	Grouse	Hake
Celeriac	Turnips	Guinea fowl	Herrings
Celery	Watercress	Hare	Lemon sole
Chicory	Wild mushrooms	Lamb	Lobsters
Chillies		Mallard	Mackerel
Fennel		Partridge	Monkfish
Garlic	Apples	Pheasant	Mussels
Horseradish	Bilberries	Rabbit	Oysters
Jerusalem artichokes	Blackberries	Turkey	Pilchards
Kale	Elderberries	Venison	Plaice
Kohlrabi	Pears	Wood pigeon	Pollack
Leeks	Quinces		Prawns
Lettuces		Clams	Red mullet
Marrows	Chestnuts	Cod	Sea bass (wild)
Parsnips	Cob nuts	Coley	Sea bream
Potatoes (maincrop)	Chives	Crab	Skate
Pumpkins	Parsley (curly)	Dab	Squid
Radishes	Rosemary	Dover sole	Turbot
Rocket	Sage	Grey mullet	Winkles
Runner beans	Sorrel		
Salad leaves	Thyme		
Salsify			

October
Week 40

M	T	W	T	F	S	S	M	T	W	T	F	S	S	M	T
3	4	5	6	7	8	9	10	11	12	13	14	15	16	17	18

3 Monday

Meal ideas

4 Tuesday

Meal ideas

5 Wednesday

Meal ideas

6 Thursday

Meal ideas

7 Friday

Meal ideas

W	T	F	S	S	M	T	W	T	F	S	S	M	T	W	T
19	20	21	22	23	24	25	26	27	28	29	30	31	1	2	3

October
Week 40

Saturday 8

Meal ideas

Sunday 9
) First Quarter

Meal ideas

Pork & Apple Burgers

❄

Butter 25g (1oz)
Eating apple 1 large, peeled and chopped
Garlic 2 cloves, peeled and crushed
Minced pork 450g (1lb)
Chopped sage 2 tbsp fresh or 1 tsp dried
Mozzarella 75g (3oz), cubed, optional
Olive oil 1 tbsp
Cheese-topped burger buns to serve
Chunky apple sauce to serve
Mixed salad leaves to serve, optional

1 Melt butter in a frying pan and fry apple and garlic for 3–4 minutes, until softened. Remove from heat and transfer to a large bowl to cool.
2 Stir in pork and sage and season to taste. Mix together thoroughly.
3 Divide mixture into four and shape into balls. If using, push mozzarella into centre, then form into burgers.
4 Heat olive oil in pan and fry burgers for 3–4 minutes on each side over a low heat until golden.
5 Serve in burger buns with apple sauce and salad, if using.

Time 20 mins   Makes 4 burgers
Calories 328 per burger
Fat 23g of which 10.1g is saturated

117

October
Week 41

10 Monday

Meal ideas

11 Tuesday

Meal ideas

12 Wednesday

Meal ideas

13 Thursday

Meal ideas

14 Friday

Meal ideas

W	T	F	S	S	M	T	W	T	F	S	S	M	T	W	T
26	27	28	29	30	31	1	2	3	4	5	6	7	8	9	10

October
Week 41

Saturday 15

Meal ideas

Sunday 16
○ Full Moon

Meal ideas

Autumn Chutney

V

Bramley cooking apples 500g (1lb 2oz), peeled, cored and chopped
Conference pears 6 large, peeled, cored and chopped
Plums 8 large, stoned and quartered
Blackberries 600g (1lb 5oz)
Ginger 50g (2oz), peeled and finely chopped
Red and green chillies 1cm (½in) piece of each, deseeded and finely chopped
Onions 600g (1lb 5oz), peeled and chopped
Granulated sugar 750g (1lb 10oz)
Distilled white wine vinegar, 5% acidity 450ml (16fl oz)

Time 3–4 hrs   Makes approx.
1.5kg (3½lb)   Calories 43 per tbsp
Fat 0g of which 0g is saturated

1 Put all ingredients into a large stainless steel preserving pan. Heat gently, stirring frequently, until mixture comes to the boil.
2 Reduce heat and cook for 3–4 hours (stirring often) until it has reduced by two-thirds, or when a wooden spoon drawn across centre leaves a path that is slow to close up.
3 Allow chutney to cool, then spoon into clean jars. Cover with acid resistant lids or waxed discs and cellophane covers.
4 Store in a cool, dark cupboard for at least 1 month before using.

October
Week 42

17 Monday

Meal ideas

18 Tuesday

Meal ideas

19 Wednesday

Meal ideas

20 Thursday

Meal ideas

21 Friday

Meal ideas

W	T	F	S	S	M	T	W	T	F	S	S	M	T	W	T
2	3	4	5	6	7	8	9	10	11	12	13	14	15	16	17

October
Week 42

Saturday 22
☾ Last Quarter

Meal ideas

Sunday 23

Meal ideas

Oriental Pork with Sweet Potato

Pork fillets 2 x 300g (11oz), trimmed
Sunflower oil 1 tbsp
**Straight-to-wok Teriyaki and
Toasted Sesame Seeds stir-fry sauce**
120g packet
Sweet potatoes 3 weighing about
1kg (2lb 3oz), peeled and chopped
Butter for mashing
Green beans 200g (7oz), trimmed

Time 45 mins   Serves 4
Calories 468 per portion
Fat 13g of which 4.7g is saturated

1 Preheat oven to 220°C/425°F/
Gas 7. Place pork fillets in a roasting
tin, drizzle with oil and roast for
10 minutes.
2 Pour stir-fry sauce over pork,
turning to coat well, and cook for a
further 15-20 minutes, basting meat
and turning once. Remove from
oven, cover with foil and leave to
stand for 5 minutes.
3 Meanwhile, simmer potatoes in a
pan of boiling water for 15 minutes
or until tender. Drain and mash with
a little butter and seasoning.
4 Cook green beans for 5 minutes in
a pan of boiling water until tender,
then drain.
5 Slice pork and set on a pile of
mash with green beans. Spoon over
pan juices and serve.

121

October
Week 43

24 Monday

Meal ideas

25 Tuesday

Meal ideas

26 Wednesday

Meal ideas

27 Thursday

Meal ideas

28 Friday

Meal ideas

W	T	F	S	S	M	T	W	T	F	S	S	M	T	W	T
9	10	11	12	13	14	15	16	17	18	19	20	21	22	23	24

October
Week 43

Saturday **29**

Don't forget to put your clocks back 1 hour tonight

Meal ideas

Sunday **30**

British Summer
Time ends
● New Moon

ORDER YOUR
KITCHEN & HOME
DIARY
2017
FREE DELIVERY
see page 149

Pumpkin & Pecan Gratin ❄

Pumpkin 1.8kg (4lb), peeled,
deseeded and cut into 2.5cm
(1in) wedges
Parmesan cheese 50g (2oz), grated
Fresh breadcrumbs 50g (2oz)
Pecan nuts 50g (2oz), chopped
Chopped thyme leaves 2 tbsp
Butter 50g (2oz), melted

1 Preheat oven to 200°C/400°F/
Gas 6. Place pumpkin in a lightly
buttered ovenproof dish. Season
well with salt and freshly ground
black pepper.
2 Mix together Parmesan cheese,
breadcrumbs, pecan nuts, thyme
and seasoning in a bowl.
3 Sprinkle evenly over pumpkin.
Then drizzle with melted butter.
4 Bake for 30–40 minutes, until
pumpkin is tender and topping is
golden. Serve immediately.

Time 50 mins   Serves 4
Calories 334 per portion
Fat 24g of which 9.5g is saturated

123

October

Week 44

M	T	W	T	F	S	S	M	T	W	T	F	S	S	M	T
31	1	2	3	4	5	6	7	8	9	10	11	12	13	14	15

31 Monday

Halloween

Meal ideas

1 Tuesday November

Meal ideas

2 Wednesday

Meal ideas

3 Thursday

Meal ideas

4 Friday

Meal ideas

W	T	F	S	S	M	T	W	T	F	S	S	M	T	W	T
16	17	18	19	20	21	22	23	24	25	26	27	28	29	30	1

November
Week 44

Saturday 5

Meal ideas

Sunday 6

Meal ideas

What's in season in November?

Artichokes	Turnips	Guinea fowl	Haddock
Beetroot	Watercress	Hare	Halibut
Butternut squash	Wild mushrooms	Lamb	Hake
Cauliflowers		Mallard	Lemon sole
Celeriac	Apples	Partridge	Lobsters
Celery	Pears	Pheasant	Mackerel
Chicory	Quinces	Rabbit	Monkfish
Horseradish		Turkey	Mussels
Jerusalem artichokes	Chestnuts	Venison	Oysters
Kale	Cob nuts	Wood pigeon	Plaice
Kohlrabi			Pollack
Leeks	Rosemary	Clams	Red mullet
Parsnips	Sage	Cod	Sea bass (wild)
Potatoes (maincrop)		Coley	Sea bream
Pumpkins	Beef	Crab	Skate
Salsify	Duck	Dab	Squid
Shallots	Goose	Dover sole	Turbot
Swedes	Grouse	Gurnard	Winkles

125

November

M	T	W	T	F	S	S	M	T	W	T	F	S	S	M	T
7	8	9	10	11	12	13	14	15	16	17	18	19	20	21	22

7 Monday
❭ First Quarter

Meal ideas

8 Tuesday

Meal ideas

9 Wednesday

Meal ideas

10 Thursday

Meal ideas

11 Friday

Meal ideas

W	T	F	S	S	M	T	W	T	F	S	S	M	T	W	T
23	24	25	26	27	28	29	30	1	2	3	4	5	6	7	8

November
Week 45

Saturday **12**

Meal ideas

Sunday **13**
Remembrance Sunday

Meal ideas

Hot Chocella

V

Milk 450ml (¾ pint)
Hazelnut chocolate spread 3 tbsp
Vanilla essence a few drops
Mini marshmallows to serve, optional

1 In a pan, heat milk with chocolate spread for a few minutes, stirring, until hot but not boiling.
2 Pour into two mugs. Add a few drops of vanilla essence and serve with marshmallows, if using.

Time 5 mins   Serves 2
Calories 231 per portion
Fat 11g of which 2.3g is saturated

127

November

Week 46

M T W T F S S M T W T F S S M T
14 15 16 17 18 19 20 21 22 23 24 25 26 27 28 29

---

14 Monday

Birthday of the Prince of Wales
○ Full Moon

Meal ideas

---

15 Tuesday

Meal ideas

---

16 Wednesday

Meal ideas

---

17 Thursday

Meal ideas

---

18 Friday

Meal ideas

W	T	F	S	S	M	T	W	T	F	S	S	M	T	W	T
30	1	2	3	4	5	6	7	8	9	10	11	12	13	14	15

November
Week 46

Saturday 19

Meal ideas

Sunday 20

Meal ideas

Raisin Parkin

V ❄

Time 1¼ hrs   Makes 20 squares
Calories 120 per portion
Fat 4g of which 2.2g is saturated

Plain flour 175g (6oz)

Oatmeal 50g (2oz)

Bicarbonate of soda 1½ tsp

Ground ginger 1 tbsp

Brown sugar 75g (3oz)

Butter 75g (3oz)

Golden syrup 50g (2oz)

Black treacle 50g (2oz)

Egg 1 medium, beaten

Milk 150ml (¼ pint)

Raisins 110g (4oz)

1 Preheat oven to 170°C/325°F/ Gas 3. Grease and line a 20cm (8in) square cake tin. Mix together flour, oatmeal, bicarbonate of soda and ground ginger.
2 Gently heat sugar, butter, syrup and treacle in a pan. Add egg and milk and mix together. Beat in dry ingredients then stir in raisins.
3 Pour into prepared tin and bake for 1 hour until firm to touch. Cool in tin, then cut into squares.

129

November
Week 47

M	T	W	T	F	S	S	M	T	W	T	F	S	S	M	T
21	22	23	24	25	26	27	28	29	30	1	2	3	4	5	6

21 Monday
☾ Last Quarter

Meal ideas

22 Tuesday

Meal ideas

23 Wednesday

Meal ideas

24 Thursday

Meal ideas

25 Friday

Meal ideas

November
Week 47

Saturday 26

Meal ideas

Sunday 27
First Sunday in Advent

Meal ideas

Petits Pots au Chocolat

V

Eggs 3 large (1 whole and 2 yolks)
Caster sugar 25g (1oz)
Single cream 300ml (½ pint)
Brandy 2 tbsp
Bittersweet dark chocolate 75g (3oz), broken into small pieces
Vanilla pod 1, cut in half lengthways, seeds scooped out
Chocolate shavings and whipped cream to decorate, optional

1 Place whole egg and egg yolks into a bowl with sugar and whisk together.
2 Pour cream and brandy into a saucepan. Add chocolate, vanilla pod and seeds, then stir over a low heat until chocolate is melted and mixture is smooth, taking care not to overheat. Remove the vanilla pod.
3 Slowly whisk chocolate cream into eggs. Strain mixture through a sieve, then pour into small heatproof pots or ramekin dishes. Cover with foil.
4 Place a wire rack inside a saucepan, then add boiling water to just below rack. Place pots on rack, cover and steam for 8-10 mins.
5 When just lightly set, allow to cool, then chill overnight. Serve topped with whipped cream and chocolate, if using.

Time 40 mins plus chilling
Serves 6   Calories 235 per portion
Fat 18g of which 9.5g is saturated

131

November

Week 48

28 Monday

Meal ideas

29 Tuesday
● New Moon

Meal ideas

30 Wednesday

St Andrew's Day

Meal ideas

1 Thursday December

Meal ideas

2 Friday

Meal ideas

December
Week 48

Saturday 3

Meal ideas

Sunday 4

Meal ideas

What's in season in December?

Beetroot	Swedes	Partridge	Langoustines
Brussels sprouts	Turnips	Pheasant	Lemon sole
Cauliflowers	Wild mushrooms	Rabbit	Lobsters
Celeriac		Turkey	Mackerel
Celery	Apples	Venison	Monkfish
Chicory	Pears		Mussels
Horseradish		Clams	Oysters
Jerusalem artichokes	Chestnuts	Cod	Plaice
Kale		Coley	Red mullet
Kohlrabi	Duck	Dab	Scallops (queen)
Leeks	Goose	Dover sole	Sea bass (wild)
Parsnips	Grouse	Gurnard	Sea bream
Potatoes (maincrop)	Guinea fowl	Haddock	Skate
Salsify	Hare	Halibut	Turbot
Shallots	Mallard	Hake	Winkles

M T W T F S S M T W T F S S M T

5 **6** **7** **8** **9** **10** **11** 12 13 14 15 16 17 18 19 20

5 Monday

Meal ideas

6 Tuesday

Meal ideas

7 Wednesday
❯ First Quarter

Meal ideas

8 Thursday

Meal ideas

9 Friday

Meal ideas

W	T	F	S	S	M	T	W	T	F	S	S	M	T	W	T
21	22	23	24	25	26	27	28	29	30	31	1	2	3	4	5

December
Week 49

Saturday 10

Meal ideas

Sunday 11

Meal ideas

Cranberry Stuffing Loaf ❄

Frozen cranberries 200g (7oz)
Caster sugar 25g (1oz)
Frozen peeled chestnuts 175g (6oz)
Onion 1, peeled and finely chopped
Chicken stock 300ml (½ pint)
Orange 1, thinly sliced
Bay leaves 2
Lincolnshire sausages 450g (1lb)
Tomato purée 1 tbsp
Cooked ham 1 thick slice, chopped
Wholemeal breadcrumbs 40g (1½oz)
Eggs 2 extra large, beaten

Time 2 hrs plus chilling
Serves 8   Calories 282 per slice
Fat 15g of which 4.4g is saturated

1 Grease a 1 litre (1¼ pint) loaf tin and line base with baking paper.
2 Cook cranberries in a small pan with sugar and 1 tbsp of water until just softened. Strain.
3 Cook chestnuts and onion in stock until just softened. Strain stock into a small pan and boil until reduced to a syrup. Arrange orange, bay leaves and a few cranberries in loaf tin.
4 Preheat oven to 190°C/375°F/Gas 5. Skin sausages and mix with purée, ham, breadcrumbs, eggs and 2 tbsp of stock. Stir in cranberries, chestnuts and onion.
5 Spoon into prepared tin, cover with foil and bake for 1¼ hours, or until juices run clear when a skewer is inserted. Cool and chill before serving.

135

December

Week 50

M T W T F S S M T W T F S S M T
12 13 14 15 16 17 18 19 20 21 22 23 24 25 26 27

---

12 Monday

Meal ideas

---

13 Tuesday

Meal ideas

---

14 Wednesday
○ Full Moon

Meal ideas

---

15 Thursday

Meal ideas

---

16 Friday

Meal ideas

W	T	F	S	S	M	T	W	T	F	S	S	M	T	W	T
28	29	30	31	1	2	3	4	5	6	7	8	9	10	11	12

December
Week 50

Saturday 17

Meal ideas

Sunday 18

Meal ideas

Forestier Pâté

Butter 150g (5oz)
Onion 1 small, peeled and finely chopped
Garlic 1 clove, peeled and crushed
Chicken livers 450g (1lb), trimmed and chopped
Mushrooms 150g (5oz), wiped and chopped
Bay leaves 2, plus extra to garnish
Dried thyme ½ tsp, plus extra to garnish
Brandy 2 tbsp
Double cream 75ml (2½fl oz)
Toast and salad to serve

Time 20 mins plus chilling
Serves 6   Calories 332 per portion
Fat 27g of which 16g is saturated

1 Melt 25g (1oz) butter and fry onion and garlic. Add livers, mushrooms, bay and thyme and season. Cover and simmer gently for 10 minutes or until livers are tender. Remove bay, then add brandy.
2 Cool slightly, transfer to a blender and whizz until smooth. Stir in cream and check seasoning.
3 Melt rest of butter and scoop off white sediment. Pour pâté into a serving dish or 6 small pots. Pour butter over, add extra bay and thyme and chill for 2–3 hours. Serve with toast and salad leaves.

December
Week 51

M	T	W	T	F	S	S	M	T	W	T	F	S	S	M	T
19	20	21	22	23	24	25	26	27	28	29	30	31	1	2	3

19 Monday

Meal ideas

20 Tuesday

Meal ideas

21 Wednesday

Winter solstice

Winter begins

(Last Quarter

Meal ideas

22 Thursday

Meal ideas

23 Friday

Meal ideas

W	T	F	S	S	M	T	W	T	F	S	S	M	T	W	T
4	5	6	7	8	9	10	11	12	13	14	15	16	17	18	19

December
Week 51

Saturday 24
Christmas Eve

Meal ideas

Sunday 25
Christmas Day

Meal ideas

Christmas Flapjacks

V ❄

Unsalted butter 175g (6oz)
Soft dark brown sugar 50g (2oz)
Golden syrup 90g (3½oz)
Rolled porridge oats 225g (8oz)
Pecan nuts 75g (3oz), chopped
Crystallised ginger 50g (2oz), chopped
Maraschino or glacé cherries 75g (3oz), quartered

Time 50 mins   Makes 12
Calories 286 per flapjack
Fat 18g of which 8.2g is saturated

1 Preheat oven to 200°C/400°F/ Gas 6. Grease a 22cm (8½in) round sandwich tin and base line with non-stick baking paper.
2 Put butter, sugar and syrup into a large saucepan and stir over a moderate heat until melted. Add all remaining ingredients and mix well. Spoon into tin and spread evenly.
3 Bake for 20-30 minutes, or until golden brown and firm to touch.
4 Allow mixture to cool slightly, run a palette knife around the edge to loosen and cut into twelve triangles. Leave until completely cold, then store in an airtight box.

139

December

M	T	W	T	F	S	S	M	T	W	T	F	S	S	M	T
26	27	28	29	30	31	1	2	3	4	5	6	7	8	9	10

26 Monday

Boxing Day

Bank Holiday, UK

Meal ideas

27 Tuesday

Bank Holiday, UK

Meal ideas

28 Wednesday

Meal ideas

29 Thursday

● New Moon

Meal ideas

30 Friday

Meal ideas

Saturday **31**
New Year's Eve

Meal ideas

January 2017 Sunday **1**
New Year's Day

Meal ideas

Hogmanay Tart

V ❄

Shortcrust pastry 225g (8oz)
Marmalade 4 tbsp
Butter 50g (2oz)
Caster sugar 50g (2oz)
Egg 1, lightly beaten
Cake crumbs 50g (2oz)
Ground cinnamon 1 tsp
Ground almonds 50g (2oz)
Raisins 110g (4oz)
Crème fraîche to serve
Orange 1, peeled and segmented, to serve

Time 45 mins   Serves 4
Calories 665 per portion
Fat 36.8g of which 14.8g is saturated

1 Preheat oven to 200°C/400°F/ Gas 6 and lightly grease a 20cm (8in) diameter flan dish.
2 Roll out pastry and place in flan dish. Spread marmalade over pastry.
3 Cream butter and sugar until light and fluffy. Then add egg, cake crumbs, cinnamon and almonds and mix well. Fold in raisins and spoon mixture into pastry case.
4 Bake for 20–25 minutes until top turns golden. Serve topped with crème fraîche and orange segments.

Thoughts and plans for 2016

Thoughts and plans for 2017

Notes

Notes

order your

new

KITCHEN & HOME

DIARY

The 2017 edition is packed with new recipes and features, and is available from September 2016

www.kitchenandhomediary.co.uk

OR

08450 948 128

Mon–Fri 9am–8pm

Quote code KH1 for

FREE DELIVERY

Home budgeting

	Opening balance	
	Income	
	New balance	

Notes	
Birthdays/Christmas	
Car insurance	
Car MOT/service/tax	
Childcare	
Clothing/shoes	
Council tax	
Dentist/optician	
Electricity	
Entertainment	
Gas/oil/solid fuel	
Groceries	
Hairdresser	
Holidays	
Home/pet insurance	
Life/medical insurance	
Mobile/phone/internet	
Mortgage/rent	
Newspapers/magazines	
Petrol/fares	
Pets	
Savings	
TV licence/satellite	
Water rates	
Other	
Other	
Other	
Other	
Other	
Other	
Other	

	Total expenditure	
	Closing balance	

February

	Opening balance	
	Income	
Notes	New balance	

Birthdays/Christmas	
Car insurance	
Car MOT/service/tax	
Childcare	
Clothing/shoes	
Council tax	
Dentist/optician	
Electricity	
Entertainment	
Gas/oil/solid fuel	
Groceries	
Hairdresser	
Holidays	
Home/pet insurance	
Life/medical insurance	
Mobile/phone/internet	
Mortgage/rent	
Newspapers/magazines	
Petrol/fares	
Pets	
Savings	
TV licence/satellite	
Water rates	
Other	
Other	
Other	
Other	
Other	
Other	
Other	

	Total expenditure	
	Closing balance	

March

	Opening balance	
	Income	
Notes	New balance	

Birthdays/Christmas	
Car insurance	
Car MOT/service/tax	
Childcare	
Clothing/shoes	
Council tax	
Dentist/optician	
Electricity	
Entertainment	
Gas/oil/solid fuel	
Groceries	
Hairdresser	
Holidays	
Home/pet insurance	
Life/medical insurance	
Mobile/phone/internet	
Mortgage/rent	
Newspapers/magazines	
Petrol/fares	
Pets	
Savings	
TV licence/satellite	
Water rates	
Other	
Other	
Other	
Other	
Other	
Other	
Other	

	Total expenditure	
	Closing balance	

April

	Opening balance	
	Income	
Notes	New balance	

Birthdays/Christmas	
Car insurance	
Car MOT/service/tax	
Childcare	
Clothing/shoes	
Council tax	
Dentist/optician	
Electricity	
Entertainment	
Gas/oil/solid fuel	
Groceries	
Hairdresser	
Holidays	
Home/pet insurance	
Life/medical insurance	
Mobile/phone/internet	
Mortgage/rent	
Newspapers/magazines	
Petrol/fares	
Pets	
Savings	
TV licence/satellite	
Water rates	
Other	
Other	
Other	
Other	
Other	
Other	
Other	

	Total expenditure	
	Closing balance	

May

	Opening balance	
	Income	
	New balance	

Notes		
Birthdays/Christmas		
Car insurance		
Car MOT/service/tax		
Childcare		
Clothing/shoes		
Council tax		
Dentist/optician		
Electricity		
Entertainment		
Gas/oil/solid fuel		
Groceries		
Hairdresser		
Holidays		
Home/pet insurance		
Life/medical insurance		
Mobile/phone/internet		
Mortgage/rent		
Newspapers/magazines		
Petrol/fares		
Pets		
Savings		
TV licence/satellite		
Water rates		
Other		
Other		
Other		
Other		
Other		
Other		
Other		

	Total expenditure	
	Closing balance	

June

Opening balance	
Income	
New balance	

Notes

Birthdays/Christmas	
Car insurance	
Car MOT/service/tax	
Childcare	
Clothing/shoes	
Council tax	
Dentist/optician	
Electricity	
Entertainment	
Gas/oil/solid fuel	
Groceries	
Hairdresser	
Holidays	
Home/pet insurance	
Life/medical insurance	
Mobile/phone/internet	
Mortgage/rent	
Newspapers/magazines	
Petrol/fares	
Pets	
Savings	
TV licence/satellite	
Water rates	
Other	
Other	
Other	
Other	
Other	
Other	
Other	

Total expenditure	
Closing balance	

July

	Opening balance	
	Income	
	New balance	

Notes	
Birthdays/Christmas	
Car insurance	
Car MOT/service/tax	
Childcare	
Clothing/shoes	
Council tax	
Dentist/optician	
Electricity	
Entertainment	
Gas/oil/solid fuel	
Groceries	
Hairdresser	
Holidays	
Home/pet insurance	
Life/medical insurance	
Mobile/phone/internet	
Mortgage/rent	
Newspapers/magazines	
Petrol/fares	
Pets	
Savings	
TV licence/satellite	
Water rates	
Other	
Other	
Other	
Other	
Other	
Other	
Other	

Total expenditure	
Closing balance	

August

Opening balance

Income

New balance

Notes

Birthdays/Christmas	
Car insurance	
Car MOT/service/tax	
Childcare	
Clothing/shoes	
Council tax	
Dentist/optician	
Electricity	
Entertainment	
Gas/oil/solid fuel	
Groceries	
Hairdresser	
Holidays	
Home/pet insurance	
Life/medical insurance	
Mobile/phone/internet	
Mortgage/rent	
Newspapers/magazines	
Petrol/fares	
Pets	
Savings	
TV licence/satellite	
Water rates	
Other	
Other	
Other	
Other	
Other	
Other	
Other	

Total expenditure

Closing balance

September

	Opening balance	
	Income	
Notes	New balance	

	Notes
Birthdays/Christmas	
Car insurance	
Car MOT/service/tax	
Childcare	
Clothing/shoes	
Council tax	
Dentist/optician	
Electricity	
Entertainment	
Gas/oil/solid fuel	
Groceries	
Hairdresser	
Holidays	
Home/pet insurance	
Life/medical insurance	
Mobile/phone/internet	
Mortgage/rent	
Newspapers/magazines	
Petrol/fares	
Pets	
Savings	
TV licence/satellite	
Water rates	
Other	
Other	
Other	
Other	
Other	
Other	
Other	

	Total expenditure	
	Closing balance	

October

	Opening balance	
	Income	
	New balance	

Notes	
Birthdays/Christmas	
Car insurance	
Car MOT/service/tax	
Childcare	
Clothing/shoes	
Council tax	
Dentist/optician	
Electricity	
Entertainment	
Gas/oil/solid fuel	
Groceries	
Hairdresser	
Holidays	
Home/pet insurance	
Life/medical insurance	
Mobile/phone/internet	
Mortgage/rent	
Newspapers/magazines	
Petrol/fares	
Pets	
Savings	
TV licence/satellite	
Water rates	
Other	
Other	
Other	
Other	
Other	
Other	
Other	

	Total expenditure	
	Closing balance	

November

	Opening balance	
	Income	
	New balance	

Notes	
Birthdays/Christmas	
Car insurance	
Car MOT/service/tax	
Childcare	
Clothing/shoes	
Council tax	
Dentist/optician	
Electricity	
Entertainment	
Gas/oil/solid fuel	
Groceries	
Hairdresser	
Holidays	
Home/pet insurance	
Life/medical insurance	
Mobile/phone/internet	
Mortgage/rent	
Newspapers/magazines	
Petrol/fares	
Pets	
Savings	
TV licence/satellite	
Water rates	
Other	
Other	
Other	
Other	
Other	
Other	
Other	

	Total expenditure	
	Closing balance	

December

	Opening balance	
	Income	
Notes	New balance	

Birthdays/Christmas

Car insurance

Car MOT/service/tax

Childcare

Clothing/shoes

Council tax

Dentist/optician

Electricity

Entertainment

Gas/oil/solid fuel

Groceries

Hairdresser

Holidays

Home/pet insurance

Life/medical insurance

Mobile/phone/internet

Mortgage/rent

Newspapers/magazines

Petrol/fares

Pets

Savings

TV licence/satellite

Water rates

Other

Other

Other

Other

Other

Other

Other

Total expenditure

Closing balance

Birthdays and anniversaries

Name	Celebration	Date

Weddings

1	Paper	14	Ivory
2	Cotton	15	Crystal
3	Leather	20	China
4	Books	25	Silver
5	Wood	30	Pearl
6	Iron	35	Coral
7	Wool	40	Ruby
8	Bronze	45	Sapphire
9	Copper	50	Gold
10	Tin	55	Emerald
11	Steel	60	Diamond
12	Silk or linen	65	Blue
13	Lace		Sapphire

Birthstones and flowers

Month	Birthstone	Flower
January	Garnet	Carnation
February	Amethyst	Violet
March	Aquamarine	Jonquil
April	Diamond	Sweet Pea
May	Emerald	Lily of the Valley
June	Pearl	Rose
July	Ruby	Larkspur
August	Peridot	Gladiolus
September	Sapphire	Aster
October	Opal	Calendula
November	Topaz	Chrysanthemum
December	Turquoise	Narcissus

Name	Celebration	Date

Year planner 2017

January		February		March	
1	Sun	1	Wed	1	Wed
2	Mon — BANK HOLIDAY	2	Thu	2	Thu
3	Tue — BANK HOLIDAY SCOTLAND	3	Fri	3	Fri
4	Wed	4	Sat	4	Sat
5	Thu	5	Sun	5	Sun
6	Fri	6	Mon	6	Mon
7	Sat	7	Tue	7	Tue
8	Sun	8	Wed	8	Wed
9	Mon	9	Thu	9	Thu
10	Tue	10	Fri	10	Fri
11	Wed	11	Sat	11	Sat
12	Thu	12	Sun	12	Sun
13	Fri	13	Mon	13	Mon
14	Sat	14	Tue	14	Tue
15	Sun	15	Wed	15	Wed
16	Mon	16	Thu	16	Thu
17	Tue	17	Fri	17	Fri — BANK HOLIDAY N IRELAND
18	Wed	18	Sat	18	Sat
19	Thu	19	Sun	19	Sun
20	Fri	20	Mon	20	Mon
21	Sat	21	Tue	21	Tue
22	Sun	22	Wed	22	Wed
23	Mon	23	Thu	23	Thu
24	Tue	24	Fri	24	Fri
25	Wed	25	Sat	25	Sat
26	Thu	26	Sun	26	Sun
27	Fri	27	Mon	27	Mon
28	Sat	28	Tue	28	Tue
29	Sun			29	Wed
30	Mon			30	Thu
31	Tues			31	Fri

April		May		June	
1	Sat	1	Mon BANK HOLIDAY	1	Thu
2	Sun	2	Tue	2	Fri
3	Mon	3	Wed	3	Sat
4	Tue	4	Thu	4	Sun
5	Wed	5	Fri	5	Mon
6	Thu	6	Sat	6	Tue
7	Fri	7	Sun	7	Wed
8	Sat	8	Mon	8	Thu
9	Sun	9	Tue	9	Fri
10	Mon	10	Wed	10	Sat
11	Tue	11	Thu	11	Sun
12	Wed	12	Fri	12	Mon
13	Thu	13	Sat	13	Tue
14	Fri BANK HOLIDAY	14	Sun	14	Wed
15	Sat	15	Mon	15	Thu
16	Sun	16	Tue	16	Fri
17	Mon BANK HOLIDAY	17	Wed	17	Sat
18	Tue	18	Thu	18	Sun
19	Wed	19	Fri	19	Mon
20	Thu	20	Sat	20	Tue
21	Fri	21	Sun	21	Wed
22	Sat	22	Mon	22	Thu
23	Sun	23	Tue	23	Fri
24	Mon	24	Wed	24	Sat
25	Tue	25	Thu	25	Sun
26	Wed	26	Fri	26	Mon
27	Thu	27	Sat	27	Tue
28	Fri	28	Sun	28	Wed
29	Sat	29	Mon BANK HOLIDAY	29	Thu
30	Sun	30	Tue	30	Fri
		31	Wed		

Year planner 2017

July		August		September	
1	Sat	1	Tue	1	Fri
2	Sun	2	Wed	2	Sat
3	Mon	3	Thu	3	Sun
4	Tue	4	Fri	4	Mon
5	Wed	5	Sat	5	Tue
6	Thu	6	Sun	6	Wed
7	Fri	7	Mon BANK HOLIDAY SCOTLAND	7	Thu
8	Sat	8	Tue	8	Fri
9	Sun	9	Wed	9	Sat
10	Mon	10	Thu	10	Sun
11	Tue	11	Fri	11	Mon
12	Wed BANK HOLIDAY N IRELAND	12	Sat	12	Tue
13	Thu	13	Sun	13	Wed
14	Fri	14	Mon	14	Thu
15	Sat	15	Tue	15	Fri
16	Sun	16	Wed	16	Sat
17	Mon	17	Thu	17	Sun
18	Tue	18	Fri	18	Mon
19	Wed	19	Sat	19	Tue
20	Thu	20	Sun	20	Wed
21	Fri	21	Mon	21	Thu
22	Sat	22	Tue	22	Fri
23	Sun	23	Wed	23	Sat
24	Mon	24	Thu	24	Sun
25	Tue	25	Fri	25	Mon
26	Wed	26	Sat	26	Tue
27	Thu	27	Sun	27	Wed
28	Fri	28	Mon BANK HOLIDAY	28	Thu
29	Sat	29	Tue	29	Fri
30	Sun	30	Wed	30	Sat
31	Mon	31	Thu		

October	November	December
1 Sun	1 Wed	1 Fri
2 Mon	2 Thu	2 Sat
3 Tue	3 Fri	3 Sun
4 Wed	4 Sat	4 Mon
5 Thu	5 Sun	5 Tue
6 Fri	6 Mon	6 Wed
7 Sat	7 Tue	7 Thu
8 Sun	8 Wed	8 Fri
9 Mon	9 Thu	9 Sat
10 Tue	10 Fri	10 Sun
11 Wed	11 Sat	11 Mon
12 Thu	12 Sun	12 Tue
13 Fri	13 Mon	13 Wed
14 Sat	14 Tue	14 Thu
15 Sun	15 Wed	15 Fri
16 Mon	16 Thu	16 Sat
17 Tue	17 Fri	17 Sun
18 Wed	18 Sat	18 Mon
19 Thu	19 Sun	19 Tue
20 Fri	20 Mon	20 Wed
21 Sat	21 Tue	21 Thu
22 Sun	22 Wed	22 Fri
23 Mon	23 Thu	23 Sat
24 Tue	24 Fri	24 Sun
25 Wed	25 Sat	25 Mon BANK HOLIDAY
26 Thu	26 Sun	26 Tue BANK HOLIDAY
27 Fri	27 Mon	27 Wed
28 Sat	28 Tue	28 Thu
29 Sun	29 Wed	29 Fri
30 Mon	30 Thu	30 Sat
31 Tue		31 Sun

Recipe index